ONE SUMMER IN MONGOLIA

FRASER McCOLL

All of the proceeds from this book are being donated to The Lotus Children's Centre in Mongolia.

ONE SUMMER IN MONGOLIA

ISBN 978-0-9562140-0-3

Published by Fraserstravel Books
10 Downs Wood
Vigo Village
Meopham
Kent DA13 0SQ

A CIP catalogue record of this book can be obtained from the British Library.

Book designed by Michael Walsh at
The Better Book Company
A division of
RPM Print & Design
2-3 Spur Road
Chichester
West Sussex
PO19 8PR

INTRODUCTION

After thirty five years of practising corporate law in London I decided, in 2007, to take a three month sabbatical. I wanted to escape from the law for a while, and spend some time working with children.

Once I had persuaded my partners to give me the time off, the question then became – where to go? I contacted various agencies that placed people of all ages in care homes and orphanages around the world, and was offered opportunities in Africa and South America. Then, through an organisation called 'Projects Abroad', I stumbled upon a placement in Mongolia, of which I knew virtually nothing. I explored the country on the Internet, and discovered that it is the least densely populated region in the world. It is larger than the United Kingdom, Germany and France put together, but with a population of only 2.8 million! Of these, about 850,000 live in the capital, Ulaanbaatar, and in the shanty towns that form its outskirts. Its neighbours are Russian Siberia to the north, China to the south and east, and Kazakhstan to the west. The southern part of the country is dominated by the great Gobi Desert, one of the most brutal and inhospitable places on earth. To the west the mountains rise as high as 4,000 metres, and cradle huge and silent lakes. However, most of the country comprises vast undulating grassland – the Central Asian Steppe.

We have all heard of the vast land empire of Chinggis Khan, which stretched from Peking (Beijing) almost to Baghdad, but since those days Mongolia fell firstly under Chinese rule until the early years of the twentieth century, and then became a Russian satellite in the Stalin years. The Russians finally ceded control in 1990 following large pro-democracy demonstrations in Ulaanbaatar. In July of that year the country became a democratic multi-party state, holding free elections.

The withdrawal of the Russians caused severe economic hardship, compounded by a series of harsh winters in the latter part of the twentieth century and early part of the twenty-first century. Between 1999 and 2002 some 11 million head of livestock died from starvation. This led to the migration of many of the nomadic herding families to the cities, where they found high unemployment and cheap vodka. Escalating levels of alcoholism and prostitution led to domestic violence, and abuse and abandonment of children. There are perhaps 4,000 street children living in Ulaanbaatar today, many of them retreating underground to the city's heating systems in the harsh winters. The temperature variations in Mongolia are dramatic – in July 2007 it touched 40°C, whereas in January 2008 temperatures plummeted to minus 44°C. Many of the people in the shanty towns live in "gers" – round felt tents known as "yurts" elsewhere. They have no running water, no electricity, no sanitary facilities, and rely for heating on ancient stoves on which they burn poor quality coal and animal dung.

I have always enjoyed remote places, had never previously been to Central Asia, and for me this was a unique opportunity. My placement was with The Lotus Children's Centre, which had been run for 13 years by Didi Kalika, an Australian yoga teacher and member of the Buddhist Ananda order. An article referring to her early work in Mongolia is reprinted in the Appendix to this book.

Didi now looks after anything between 120 and 150 children in Yarmag, a shanty town on the outskirts of Ulaanbaatar. She also runs a primary school close to the Centre, and a vegetarian café which provides work for some of the Lotus school leavers as well as much needed funds for Lotus. There is a "mini Lotus" in Erdenet, a town six hours drive to the north of Ulaanbaatar, where Didi provides a home for another 17 children. She receives no state aid at all, and therefore relies exclusively on private donations to fund the organisation. Life is a permanent struggle for financial survival. Despite this, and the desperate background from which many of the children come, the atmosphere is happy, positive, and caring. The children are encouraged to rediscover their self esteem, to learn respect for each other and the house-mothers who look after them, and to develop their talents.

For me, this was supposed to be a three month break from the law, after which I would return happily to private practice. It has not worked out like that. It was the most rewarding experience of my life. I fell in love with both Mongolia and its people, and especially the children and staff at Lotus. On my return to England I formed a UK charity, The Lotus Children's Centre Charitable Trust, which is a vehicle not only for raising money, but also for raising awareness of the plight of the Mongolian street children.

My return to Lotus in 2008 was highly emotional – the children reacting to my return with love and affection.

I spent most of my time in Mongolia working in a summer camp with the children, and living in a ger. I recorded my thoughts in a notebook daily, and each time I returned to the city I kept in touch with my family and friends by writing up those notes on a blog. After I had been in Mongolia for just three weeks on my first visit, my good friend Brian wrote in a comment on the blog "*And you think you can just go back to the law? You will never get these kids out of your head*". Brian was right. They have become a part of my life, and I shall return to see them every year.

This book records my blog exactly as I wrote it at the time. I have only altered it to correct mistakes, and add some background for the sake of clarity.

SUMMER 2007

1 – THE FIRST WEEK – ULAANBAATAR

June 3 – Morning

I arrived in Ulaanbaatar, the capital of Mongolia, about two hours ago, after flying down from Moscow in an ancient Soviet jet. The flight was chaotic – there was almost no room for hand luggage, so most people just had to stuff it under their seats. It also had the least leg room of any plane I have ever been on! The road in to the city from the airport was littered with potholes, and the whole place has the feel of a third world country, as I expected. It's cold here – about 1 degree as we landed, but a beautiful clear sky, and the sun is shining brightly.

For the first four nights I am staying at the Chinggis Guest House, which is a bit like a youth hostel at home. But I do have my own room, with shared use of a toilet and rather primitive shower. The place is clean, and the owner speaks some English, and is very helpful. She insisted on giving me Mongolian bread and jam, and black tea, for breakfast!

This afternoon I have my induction and a tour of the city to attempt to orientate myself. Tomorrow I meet the children at the orphanage, and start work.

June 3 – Afternoon

Just had a tour round the city with Ariuna, my desk officer (sounds a bit like MI6!). Very windy and dusty, but bright and now warm. We ate in a Mongolian cafe, where I was the only westerner, and I was treated to what was described to me as an exotic delicacy, which turned out to be potato salad! I also drank traditional tea, with butter and salt, which was pretty disgusting. I discovered very shortly afterwards that I had no immediate need for the herbal laxative that I was told to take with me...

June 4

Yesterday evening I went into the park to listen to my ipod for a couple of hours. It is very stark there and quite dreary with no grass or flowers. I was sitting there quite happily listening to a classic episode of Alan Partridge, when three children came up to me and dumped the smallest on my lap! Clearly they wanted money, but Ariuna had told me not to encourage begging so I had to shoo them away. I walked back to the Guest House at about 7pm. On the way I felt something by my side and there was a kid in the process of lifting my phone from the pocket of my fleece. He'd managed to unzip it without my noticing! I was very lucky not to lose it, but will be much more careful from now on. I've been down to the orphanage today, but I'll write about that separately, as all the letters on this computer are in the Mongolian Cyrillic script (the same alphabet as Russia) and not in English. It's taking me for ever to write anything, as I can't touch type!

June 5

That's better – the PC at the other place was pretty hopeless. I've just had to send a mail from my address for a French doctor who is working as a volunteer in the womens' hospital, and doesn't speak any English or Mongolian! She wanted to send a message to her husband to say she had arrived safely, so she dictated it to me in French and I wrote it on the Cyrillic PC – the blind leading the blind!

I went to the children's home this morning. It is located in Yarmag, a suburb of the city, in what is not much more than a shanty town. There are about 150 kids there, but some of them are young adults, as they range from newborn to 20. Some of the older ones have special needs, and there is no adult centre for them to go on to, so they will now have to stay at Lotus indefinitely. The director is an Australian woman (Didi Kalika) who founded it about 13 years ago when she took in seven or eight children from the street, and it simply grew from there. It is called The Lotus

Children's Centre. The kids live in family units each with about 8 or 10 children, looked after by a house mother. Most of the units are in low houses built of straw bricks, but a couple are in gers (yurts). There is no water on site – it has to be fetched in barrels from a stand-pipe about a quarter of a mile away. The toilets are just dug in one corner of the play yard, and there are no facilities for the disposal of rubbish. All pretty basic!

It was an introductory day today, so I only stayed about three hours, but I took a dozen of the boys on to some waste land adjoining the home, and organised a football match. Some of them played in bare feet, although there were sharp stones everywhere, and what on examination appeared to be a camel's foot, no longer attached to its owner, but which delighted the local flies! A couple of kids from outside the orphanage joined in wearing their football shirts – one was 'Riise' and the other 'Kaka'. They had expensive looking trainers, but notwithstanding the kit they weren't as good as my lads!

After football we had lunch – rice with some potato and scraps of vegetable followed by more Mongolian tea with butter and salt. I seem to have retained this lot, so maybe I'm already getting used to it! I then took the bus back into town, as I had to register with the immigration authorities as an overseas worker. The best news of the day is that I wandered about getting my bearings and found somewhere that sells Earl Grey tea – so I'm off there right now! If there's anyone still reading, there'll be more tomorrow.

June 6

Today I had to find my own way to the orphanage on the bus – not as easy as it sounds, because very few signs are in English, and only Mongolians use the ancient and absurdly overcrowded buses – I am always the only westerner on it. They all tend to look at me rather oddly! Anyway, I'd memorised it okay, so got there and back safely. From early June to about mid-August most of the children live in gers in a summer camp which is set up by Lotus in Terelj –

an attractive valley about 80 kilometres from Ulaanbaatar ('UB'). It gives the children some space to do outdoor activities, and an opportunity to escape for a while from the grime of Yarmag.

Most of today was spent organising toys, books and equipment for the Camp. I've been designated English teacher for the summer, and as what I know about teaching could be tattooed on the back of an ant, that should be interesting! I could do with Sarah (my daughter) here, as she is a teacher in a special school...

I've made a friend in a young lad called Umesh who asked me yesterday, and again today, would I be coming back tomorrow? You'll gather from this that he speaks a little English, so with luck he will improve a bit while I'm here. Four new kids arrived today, one a tiny baby. She only weighed about four pounds, but seems to be quite strong. Didi, who is a yoga teacher, and member of the Buddhist 'Ananda' order, has far too much to do to fit into the hours of daylight. However, she is getting help planning the summer camp from a French woman who works for Save the Children.

It's not that I'm obsessed with my stomach, but lunch today was mashed potato, rice and some strips of cabbage! The Lotus diet is strictly vegetarian. As a result, I renewed with enthusiasm a search I started yesterday for a bar called Dave's Place, a hang out of the Embassy guys and other sundry Brits. I'm going there now (and probably tomorrow also) to get a couple in before I go down to the Camp, where anything resembling western food or drink will be conspicuous by its absence.

June 7

Took the bus again this morning. There is always music on, and there is a singer I've heard several times now with quite a good tenor voice, who is a dead ringer for Donny Munro singing in Gaelic (google him, those who don't know...).

Another day today gathering stuff for the Camp – getting about 100 children to a summer camp for three months is a huge logistical task. My shadow (Umesh) followed me around, so he and I read together for a while. He can read English better than he can speak it, unless maybe it's a lack of confidence. Anyway, he's reciprocating, and trying (with not much luck so far) to teach me some basic Mongolian. I'm told he's 16, although he looks much younger than that as he is very small. He likes football more than anything else in the world, so I'm going to indoctrinate him into supporting The Eagles!! There is also a special needs boy who has tagged on to me, although I can't yet pronounce his name, and he speaks hardly a word. But he does like books, so we've just been leafing through them together.

In the Guest House today I met Caroline, a French teacher, who visited the orphanage, and also helped me upload some photos onto my blog.

Amazingly hot here now – it was 1 degree when I arrived, and 35 today! But the humidity is about zero, so it's easy enough to cope with. The real problem is the dust – in the spring strong winds blow the dust up from the Gobi, and apparently a lot of animals die. Summer has just started, but the wind is still there, only lighter, and the dust makes me cough a lot.

Tonight I'm having dinner with some other volunteers down here – a couple of doctors, and some other guys working in schools or orphanages. Tomorrow I'm going to be driven to the summer camp by Cecile, the French woman from Save the Children, to see how things are going. I expect to go down there permanently on Friday or Saturday.

Someone died today in the district where Lotus is located, and the children were given chocolate and fizzy drinks by the deceased's relatives. That is the tradition following a death – I have been here just five days and there have been two already. Nobody seemed very sad, and I guess that is because as Buddhists they believe that the person will come back in a more enlightened state than in their previous life. So in many ways it is an occasion for rejoicing.

Most of the children have now gone down to the Camp, and I shall be following them shortly. Sadly the young special needs boy (Ariumbata) will not be coming. I'm not quite sure why, but he will certainly miss all the others, as only the little ones will be left, and it will isolate him even more. I'm sure I will be back a couple of times at least, so I will visit him then, as he hardly leaves my side now when I am there.

June 8 – Friday (I think)

You lose track of the day here, as it really doesn't matter which day of the week it is. The routine is the same: up at about 7, breakfast (I brought some porridge with me), and then the bus to the orphanage. Lunch of rice or noodles plus potato, plus (on a good day) bits of cabbage or carrots; and back on the bus to the city at about 4. Then begins the hunt for something decent to eat/drink in the evening. I've got that sorted now, and have found a couple of places (plus Dave's) which serve good cheap food, so all is well with my stomach, whose well known cast iron qualities are serving me well.

Not much happening at Lotus today, as almost all the over threes have gone down to the Camp. Umesh is amongst the last to go (tomorrow) so I read with him for a bit, and then we kicked a football around. My Mongolian is rubbish, I guess I only know about 10 words, but I can get by on those, plus bits of English, plus sign language. I have to say I am very relaxed – the stresses are very different from those in the office, and it is a relief not to have any clients chasing me – for the first time in 35 years!

Caroline, whom I mentioned yesterday, has been cycling across Asia on her own. She went across Vietnam, Cambodia and Laos, then found her way up through China into Inner Mongolia, crossed the Gobi desert, and has now left UB for northern Mongolia and

Siberia. She will work her way west across Russia to Moscow, and then do the easy bit and cycle back to Paris! Apparently the track across the Gobi was a bit like the rough, stony tracks in central Australia, and she camped in the desert. She said that she wasn't worried as she was on the main route from the south up to UB, so at least 3 or 4 vehicles passed her each day! On the way she is trying to visit schools and childrens' homes in each location, and is writing a blog which is read by her own class at home. The kids in the orphanage did some wonderful drawings for her. You can meet some extraordinary people in this world.

June 9

Just had my first dose of the dreaded UB Squits (those of a sensitive nature log off now!) I had just settled down in the Post Office for an hour pre-paid (all of 60 cents) on the Internet, when my stomach did the much feared triple salchow. Recognising the symptoms from a joyful moment when trekking in Nepal, I knew I had two choices – the paperless toilet of the bar next door, or the 15 minute (12 if I shifted) walk with buttocks firmly clenched to the Guest House. I chose the latter, and made it with moments to spare...serves me right for boasting yesterday of my cast iron guts.

I waited in the Guest House for half an hour (listening to Blackadder on my ipod) in case there were any after-shocks, and have now invested a further 60 cents in the Mongolian Post Office.

I'd had lunch in Millie's Cafe, a well-known haunt of expats, and pretty safe for its food, but it could have been the raw tomato with the scrambled egg that did it. Anyway I met an interesting American guy there who is a freelance economist travelling to fairly obscure locations in the world and giving (as he put it) vague economic advice for fees sufficient to enable him to continue travelling. Not a bad life.

There is a German couple staying in the Guest House, who had a rucksack stolen in a restaurant on Thursday evening. They lost one passport, containing his Russian visa, plus cash, their rail tickets to Irkutsk, and (worst of all) their camera with 1,000 photos on it. Some of them they had uploaded on to the Net, but the rest were lost. They had been travelling already for three months, and were desperately sad to lose so many photographs. Amazingly, everything else has been sorted out – the German embassy replaced his passport, and the Russian embassy renewed the visa – all in the space of 24 hours! I'm quite sure it would never happen so fast in London.

Tonight I'm meeting Del (who is teaching here) and we are going to plan a four day trip down to the Gobi Desert. I've been warned by Cecile that being with the kids 24/7 will be hard going, and that I should take more breaks, so we will go in about three weeks. Then I am staying with Ivan Elliott in his hotel (sharing his room) for a couple of nights from 10 July so that we can go to the Naadam Festival together. This is the main sporting festival in the Mongolian calendar, and involves the three "manly sports" of wrestling, archery, and horse racing on long straight courses outside the city. I am told that vast amounts of vodka are consumed. Ivan is a friend and client who, when I told him about my sabbatical a month or so ago, decided on an impulse to spend a couple of weeks in Mongolia in July. Good for him!

There is a massive disparity of wealth here. In the city centre you can see expensive cars (I am told there are three Mercedes sports cars in UB!), and well dressed people strolling about at night going to bars and restaurants. The young girls seem to want to expose as much flesh as possible (I just look the other way...) and some of the young men are brash and arrogant. But outside the city centre, there is awful poverty, as in the district where Lotus is. I suppose this contrast is typical of the emerging ex-Soviet satellites.

I've not been to the orphanage at all today, and strangely miss it. I quite like to get away from the downtown poseurs, and am looking forward to my first stint at the summer camp tomorrow – although I have to confess I am a little apprehensive, as I will be living in a ger the whole time, and will be a long way from the comfort of English voices. It was Adrian at the office who said we should come out of our comfort zones from time to time...

It will take about three hours to drive to the camp, the last 15 minutes off road. So this will be my last blog for at the very least three weeks, and maybe until the 10 July. I'll try to take lots of photos to send back next time.

2 – THE FIRST SPELL IN SUMMER CAMP

To my surprise and delight I'm back in UB for a two night break. That seems to be the norm even for the Mongolians in the Camp so that they can see their families, get a shower, etc. Conditions there are very basic indeed. I went there with Cecile, who was spending the day helping to set up the Camp. She is very concerned and frustrated at the apparent lack of preparation and basic hygiene. The Camp is close to the river, and the kids wash and clean their teeth in it. The water is also used for cooking and washing up – sometimes properly boiled, sometimes not. The problem is that the river is badly polluted by cattle and other animals. as well as humans. As Cecile graphically put it: "*The kids wash themselves in shit*". Many of them have nasty skin problems, and those same kids help to prepare the food, as well as wash the dishes. It'll be a miracle if I survive without getting sick sometime...but I did take twelve litres of water with me to wash with, clean my teeth, and to drink. Having said that, I do drink the Mongolian tea that they make as I think it would be a slight not to, and (believe it or not) I am getting used to it.

So here is my diary for the last eight days:-

June 10

Cecile and I arrived in the Camp in the middle of a dust storm which soon turned to thunder and lightning and heavy rain. The Camp was not yet complete, and Cecile and I struggled to cover up the exposed felt of gers that had not yet been erected – if the felt becomes wet it is useless.

As my ger was not yet ready, I was shown into that of Enkhee, the Camp Manager, who was to share one of the other gers for my first few nights.

Having settled in I walked over to the cooking ger and watched the evening meal being prepared by children with snotty noses and dirty hands!

I also checked out the toilet facilities, which were the worst I have ever seen – much worse than when I visited my son Andrew in Africa, because the pit is too shallow. About three feet deep, and nowhere near enough for about 100 people for three months! Cecile and I decided to re-dig the toilet the following morning, and also to dig a rubbish tip.

June 11

The day started with the children gathering in a circle in the middle of the Camp, and doing some simple stretching exercises. After that Enkhee announced the activities for the day, and then a desultory attempt was made to clean the Camp. I discovered that this pattern is followed every morning, but the Camp is always filthy, partly because there is no perimeter fence and the nomads' cattle wander into it all the time and seem to prefer it even to the river as their chosen toilet.

After breakfast, which was some sort of milky porridge concoction, many of the children played down by the river. One boy of about 11 gashed his toe almost to the bone, and it poured blood. Nobody nearby seemed to take much notice, and I had to do my best to try to clean and bandage it. It must have been really painful, but there was no sign of any tears.

June 12

I moved to my new ger, which has now been erected, but which is very cold and unfriendly. Basically, it is a round wooden base (with plenty of gaps in it), and attached to that is a light wooden trellis which is stretched around the base. The felt is attached to the trellis, and on top of that is a canvas cover. There is an aperture in the roof to let in the light, covered by plastic on the inside to keep out the rain. The only furniture is a wooden cabinet, a small table and one stool. I sleep in my sleeping bag on a dirty mattress on the floor.

It was warmer today, after a very cold day yesterday, and in the afternoon I did some teaching with the children, although they do not appear to be very interested!

I found an ancient copy of the English language "UB Post" in the cooking ger, and read that a three year international study by academics has concluded that Chinggis Khan had an IQ of 204! Mongolians are obsessed with their pride in him and all the men claim to be descendants of his! He is on no account to be criticised.

By the end of the day I was feeling pretty dirty already, as I am unshaven and have only washed my face. I have not been able to bring myself to use the pit toilet, and instead deployed the skills I had learned from reading the book "How to Shit in the Woods"!

In the evening I played some ball games with the children, but unfortunately managed to kneel in some cow dung. I don't have a spare pair of trousers with me (only my shorts), and will therefore have to put up with this for the next week!

Sadly, Umesh has not been able to come to the Camp after all, as he suffers from severe epilepsy, and it is considered too much of a risk for him to be so far from any medical help.

I have found the children very demanding today, and there is no escape from them. By the end of the day I was very tired and feeling slightly melancholic.

June 13

In the morning I took some children for a short walk, and then did some skipping games with them and played football. Surprisingly (notwithstanding the almost non-existent hygiene facilities) the food is okay – the diet comprises primarily cabbage, carrots, potatoes, pasta and rice. This is supplemented with various dairy products, including milk, yoghurt and cream. The dairy products are acquired from a Kazakh family who live in a ger further up the valley, tending to their cattle. I went there to collect some milk in the afternoon. They allow the calves to suckle the cattle to bring the milk in, and then hand milk them from a stool, working on two teats at once. I have hand milked before when I owned a smallholding, but they are far more skilful than I ever was!

In the evening I attempted to adjourn again to the woods, but having discovered that the only slightly secluded area was occupied by some Mongolian campers, I relented, took a deep breath, and used the communal pit. However, good did come of the encounter with the Mongolian campers, as they called me over, and shared with me some cherries, some dried fruit and (best of all) a big slug of wonderfully pure vodka. I slept well that night!

June 14

I finally made a serious attempt today to instil a basic knowledge of spoken English in some of the older children. They appear to be able to read English quite well, but it turns out that although they can pronounce English words, in most cases they don't know what they mean at all. They have been taught to recognise the pronunciation of words, but not their meaning – which is of little use! However, some of them are clearly very bright, and given the right opportunities could learn quickly.

Today's class was attended by eight of the 12 year olds, plus two ger mothers. We did colours and numbers for about 45 minutes. They seemed to enjoy it, and I will now be teaching each morning.

Afterwards I prepared a lesson plan for the next three days from a book which I found in the Lotus Primary School. It is really designed to teach English to overseas students, but is still of some help.

In the afternoon I had a long conversation, through Enkhee, with a little boy of about nine. When he was six or seven his mother, who was the victim of violent abuse from his dad, had to give him up because she had no job and no money. He remembers this, and is prepared to talk about it. He knows his mum's name, and would like to find her again. He talked a lot, and asked detailed, intelligent, questions about my job, my family and my life. He told me that when he grows up he would like to go to university, and then to marry, and live a proper family life with his wife and children. He asked me how often I saw my children, if they live with me, and what they did for a living. I told him about Sarah's partner Steve, and his police dogs, and he asked what happened to the dogs when they were too old to work. His ambition is to visit other countries with his family, and he hopes that he and I can meet again when is grown up, and said that he wishes I was staying beyond August. He is bright and mature for his age, and appears very caring. It was the most interesting conversation I have had since I arrived in Mongolia, and made me feel less lonely. His name is Uurganaa.

June 15

Yesterday evening we finally filled in the old toilet pit and dug a new one. This is twice the depth of the original, but still won't last too long with over 100 people using it every day! However it is progress of a sort...

The maintenance worker and the driver from Lotus came this morning in a pick-up to build a simple fence around the site. By the end of the day it was two-thirds finished, and when complete it should at least prevent the nomads' cattle and goats from roaming through the Camp.

Yesterday was cold and windy, but today proved to be calm, sunny and hot. The new pit is already full of flies and bluebottles, which assault the squatter as soon as he bears his bottom! Reckon I will use the woods again tomorrow!

In the English classes I have discovered that one young girl who is aged 11 or 12 is very bright, which helps me to communicate with the class as a whole. We played a "guess what object I am thinking of" game. One member of the class had to think of an object in the ger, and the others had to guess what he/she was thinking of by asking questions, in English. I think they enjoyed it, but I shall soon be running out of lesson plan ideas...

In the afternoon a lot of the children went swimming, and some of them did yoga with one of the ger mothers. At 4.00 p.m. (yoghurt time) I went to the kitchen ger, and some of my English students tried to teach me to make pastry-filled balls stuffed with potato, rice and vegetables. They (quite rightly) laughed at my ineptitude!

A Mongolian guy (the only other man in the Camp) arrived a couple of nights ago. He doesn't speak English, but Enkhee told me he is the music teacher, and his name is Zorig. He was picking at his guitar last night, and I wandered into his ger. He sang a couple of songs from the Gobi, his homeland, and then asked me to join in. I obliged with "Blowin' in the Wind". Zorig knew the song and we sang it together. He in Mongolian, me in English. It seemed quite bizarre to hear Dylan's best known song sung in an English/Mongolian duet in the heart of the Central Asian Steppe!

June 16

It was raining hard when we woke up this morning, and we were all reluctant to emerge from our gers. For breakfast we had some dried dates to go with the rice milk. Yippee! I have to say that the concept of eating rice milk for breakfast every day until the end of August is not deeply attractive!

After the English lesson I attempted (but failed) to mend the door to my ger, which is leaning erratically. I discovered that all of the Camp tools were in Enkhee's ger, which is locked as she is away for the day. Instead I laid a strip of linoleum in my ger which made it ever so slightly more homely. After lunch Uurganaa came to my ger and asked to do some English reading. We browsed through a couple of books, and I then showed him my ipod and introduced him to Queen – we sat on the floor of the ger singing "We will rock you" (when he sang it later in the Camp one of the other children, either by accident or design, got the wrong idea and started singing at the top of his voice "We will f**k you"!)

In the early evening I decided to tackle one of the hills behind the Camp – a ridge probably about 700 feet above us. I had walked about 400 yards when Uurganaa caught me up so I let him come with me. There are stunning mountain views from the top – it is a very wild and lonely country. I don't think Uurganaa had been up there before. At one point he claimed to see a bear but I think (hope) it was his imagination. He has an open, friendly, honest face and is desperate to learn. I will have to be careful not to be dominated by him.

Tomorrow is Sunday, and I can open Sarah's Fathers Day card at last! I have been waiting for that...

June 17

Fathers Day! And so far removed from home it felt very strange. However tomorrow I shall be going back to Ulaanbaatar for a brief break, which will give me an opportunity to use the Internet, and ring home.

In the afternoon I took two more of the children up into the hills. We walked for longer than I had done with Uurganaa – about two hours, and both children had fun. I have decided to take a small group each afternoon, as I feel good on the hills, and so do they. The hillsides are pristine – beautiful, pure and remote – and in complete contrast to the rubbish and dirt that tends to surround the ger encampments that are dotted around the valley. The nomads who live in the gers don't own any land, they simply pitch their encampments where they want, until the grazing for their cattle/sheep/goats runs out, and they then move on, leaving their rubbish behind.

We met nobody when walking and you get the feeling of being where very few have walked before. I am now tempted by a ridge I could see from today's walk, which I guess would be a round trip of maybe three hours. I will take some of the older children on that. The kids really seem to enjoy it – I don't think they have done anything like it before, and I feel I may have a useful role to play in taking them out of their everyday environment and showing them something different. Or is that just a romantic notion? Perhaps…

June 18

Reflecting on my first spell in the Camp, the hardest thing was the isolation. Only Enkhee speaks any English, and that is very basic. It is difficult to live without any real communication. In a comment on my blog Brian had warned me about becoming melancholic, and he was right, but I will now be coming back to the city every seven or eight days, so I will have more access to the outside world then I expected. Which is good.

Having showered, and washed my hair and filthy clothes, I met up with Del to make some firm plans for our trip to the Gobi. I am told you can fly, but we would rather go by jeep even though it takes a couple of days. Apart from anything else, the Lonely Planet warns against using any of the internal Mongolian airlines, which apparently have a bad safety record. I had planned to eat a large burger and chips as soon as I got back into the city but, strangely, I have already become used to the vegetarian diet, and Del and I ended up in a small café eating ratatouille and drinking local beer.

June 19

A very quick note as I am off back to the Gulag – sorry, Summer Camp – again in 10 minutes. I guess under Soviet rule the word "Gulag" would have been monitored, and this site closed down. Hope it doesn't happen now...actually the Communists remain very popular here. There is a huge statue of Lenin in the City, and people say that whilst there was less wealth for the few in Communist times, everyone had a job, and there was a basic living to be had by all. The conversion to a market economy is very painful for some. I cannot judge whether it is worth it or not.

Two events in Mongolia this week you will not have heard about at home – the first was a helicopter crash in the west with many deaths. As I said yesterday, the LP advises against using any internal flights. The second was that I was told by some VSO volunteers staying in the Guest House for a conference, that in the town in the north where they are living a Siberian tiger was seen yesterday. It is the largest big cat in the world, and whilst it is now a protected species and the numbers are up to about 550, this was still a very rare sighting.

My time has run out. Back next week...

3 – THE SECOND SPELL IN SUMMER CAMP

So here I am back at the Chinggis Guest House after another eight day stint at the Summer Camp. There is quite a lot to report, and I have written notes, so I will try to summarise each day since I was last in UB. Here goes...

June 20

I got back to the Camp at about 4:30, having visited en route a young American, Ramsay, who is living with a nomad family for two months. The head of the family, in whose ger Ramsay is staying, has 16 children, and cannot remember how many grandchildren! They all apparently come and go the whole time, so there is a constant stream of people passing through his small camp. Ramsay's duties involve cleaning out the calf pens, building fencing, and generally assisting with the animals. On the day I saw him he had helped remove the equivalent of two wisdom teeth from a horse (with a hammer and chisel!), and had held a sheep while it was slaughtered. They don't cut the throat and bleed the sheep in Mongolia, but instead they make a small incision near the heart, put their hand in and twist, and the sheep dies instantly. It may not sound very nice, but is probably better then the methods we use, as the sheep suffers only momentarily. Ramsay's ger is about a kilometre up the valley from where I am, so I may wander down and visit sometime.

It was a gala day in the Camp, and all the children took part in drawing, singing and dancing competitions. Didi was staying over, and after dark we lit a bonfire and there was Mongolian dancing by the children in costume, and singing to the guitar of the music teacher, Zorig. Thought about Dad, who would have been 91 that day, and who would have been avidly following the blog.

June 21

In English we did months, days of the week, and seasons. We also played a game where the children had to write down their favourite month, fold up the paper, and then give it to me. I opened them one by one, and they had to guess who had chosen that particular month. The person who chose it then had to explain why he/she had chosen that month. All in English. They did pretty well.

After lunch I took Ankhar, a rather difficult lad who is not well liked by the other children, for a walk in the hills. It was hot, and he whinged a bit, but I had taken an orange drink for him, and he managed alright. I had a snooze in my ger after that, and then chatted by the river with some of the kids and with Nyamaa, one of the ger mothers, who I have discovered does speak some simple English. She told me that some of the children had very sad backgrounds. One of them had witnessed his mum's boyfriend stabbing her to death. He was apparently so traumatised that he stopped growing. On Nyamaa's small wage she has to keep her mother, who has a bad heart, and her grandfather. She does not know who her father was, but believes he was Russian. She has had no boyfriends "*because I am fat*", and the children make up songs about her weight.

June 22

Tremendous gale force winds last night. I was a bit concerned about the structure of the ger, which was shaking dramatically. There is a rope you are supposed to tie to something in a storm, but I didn't know to what! Some of the children were frightened, and cried, but we all survived. The morning was hot. One of my favourite kids is Galaa, who is 19, and special needs, but always with a smile on his face, and not at all demanding of my attention. I encourage him to come to English, although he doesn't really contribute much. On this morning he was very burnt about the shoulders and back, and was just wearing a cut away vest, so was burning more the whole time. The ger mothers don't seem to notice this sort of thing. I gave him one of my 'Trek Peru' tee-shirts to wear, which he did for the next three days with great pride! He kept coming up to me, pointing to his shirt, and saying "*English*".

Mongolians have little or no body hair, and so the kids are fascinated with the hair on my legs. They keep wanting to stroke it, and sometimes to pull it out!

There was a government camp inspection this afternoon (I am surprised and pleased that they have such things), and they spoke to all of us and interviewed some of the children separately. Very thorough. They were apparently happy with most things (including the English teacher!), but want to do tests of the water (quite right), and have also insisted that we double the depth of the pit toilets (also quite right).

June 23

Good news! Del arrived to stay overnight in my ger, together with an American student, Hanson, who is working in the US funded orphanage in UB, which is apparently very well equipped. It was good to see them, as we could talk English together. We walked in the hills on our own after lunch, and just chatted. When we got back I discovered that Del used to play semi-pro football, so he and I organised a game with the boys. He is really good, and became an instant hero with the kids, and I have now gone well downhill in their eyes by comparison! However, some of the boys are highly talented, and when one of them first gave Del the "Cruyff Turn", and then nutmegged him, I felt a whole lot better!

Didi also arrived, with an Aussie friend (Bratatii), who is helping in connection with the proposed relocation of Lotus to a new site on the other side of town. So the Camp was suddenly full of English speakers which was very relaxing.

I chatted to Del and Hanson in my ger after dark, and Hanson told me more about the orphanage in which he is working. It is funded and run by American Baptists, and is clearly the height of luxury compared to Lotus. However, there is a very strong religious component to it, with compulsory hymns and prayers each day. Hanson's view is that there is an element of indoctrination of the children in the Baptist faith, and he has considerable doubts about this in what is essentially a Buddhist country.

June 24

Del and Hanson got up at 4:30 to climb the hill behind the Camp and watch the sun rise. I stayed in my sleeping bag! Didi then suggested that the five of us (she, Bratatii, me, Del and Hanson) visit a monastery further down the Terelj valley. It took us about an hour off road in Didi's four-wheel drive car, and then we had to climb. It was a lovely setting and we sat for a while and meditated. Didi then found a shop she knew of nearer to the Camp, and we bought 100 ice creams for the kids (and one each for us – a great treat!)

Del and Hanson went back in a jeep to UB before dinner, and after they had gone Bratatii showed me lots of photos on her laptop of an ayervedic clinic and school for destitute children in India, with which she is closely involved. She still spends much of her time there, and offered me a teaching job! I told her that was out of the question in the immediate future, but maybe one day, provided Brenda could come as well and teach yoga. She thought that might be a possibility. We shall see. The clinic is very interesting, and is available primarily for the local tribal people. The principle technique is acupuncture, and seems to be very successful. The atmosphere there looks lovely.

June 25

Took an English class in the morning with about nine of the older kids, and then went for a long walk with them and Nyamaa. We tramped through the forest, crossing several streams, towards the ridge of mountains in the distance. At one point we reached a stream which was quite deep and very muddy, and the first child who tried to cross lost her shoe in the mud. I tried to fish it out, but couldn't find it. We thought we might have to abandon the walk, but, quite by chance, we found another shoe which (almost) fitted, and I went upstream to look for a better crossing point. Eventually I found a fallen log, and we used this as a bridge, and all safely crossed. I (briefly) attained hero status as a result, and the kids started to call me Tarzan! (no Jane here, sadly...). After about an hour and a half we reached the foot of the ridge, and most of the kids, as well as Nyamaa, wanted to climb to the top. So did I really, but we had Galaa with us, who doesn't have a very good sense of balance (he fell right into one of the streams, but just giggled as usual!). It would have been dangerous to try to get him to the top as it is quite precipitous, so I towed him as far as I could and then waited with three other children for the rest to get up and down. We didn't get back to Camp until the middle of the afternoon, and for much of the rest of the day I just read and relaxed (when the kids allowed!). In the evening, the couple who live in the adjoining ger (she is an ex-Lotus girl) wandered in, and I was given the baby to cuddle. Obviously accepted!

June 26

The food/lack of hygiene finally got me and on a short walk I suddenly felt my rear end about to explode. I made a feeble attempt to hide behind a rock which was only about a foot high, and duly let rip. I felt pretty bad, and had another emergency twenty minutes later back in the Camp, but this time I did get to the pit. Took Imodium for the first time and declined the camp food for the rest of the day. Had a biscuit, a nectarine, and a bit of dried fruit I had been saving. Probably shouldn't have had the fruit, but got away with it.

I rested for a few hours, and then decided to take Galaa for a walk up one of the nearer, and less steep, hills, so he could see what it was like to get to the top. He was pleased about this, but unfortunately we were joined by Ariumbata who, to my surprise, had come down to the Camp a few days previously. He is very strong and quite difficult, and couldn't be persuaded to turn back. In the end what were now three of us were joined by one of the younger kids, and also a little girl of about nine who is quite bright, but suffers from cerebral palsy, and is very unsteady on her feet. So we just wandered along the valley for a bit, and then came back. Nyamaa (whose English is now more confident) told me that Ariumbata is very sexually aware, and was found kissing one of the older special needs girls. She thinks he may become a danger to the younger ones, and then said "*Perhaps he'll die*". They have a different attitude to life and death, possibly because they see so much tragedy. I was told by Bratatii that the previous winter four of the Lotus children had gone to the local state hospital suffering from a viral infection, and all four had died. She said that she personally had seen bodies in the corridors of the hospital being eaten by maggots. That doesn't happen immediately after death. Fortunately for us wealthy westerners there is a private clinic in UB staffed by American and Dutch doctors, so if we get sick, that's where we would go. Of course it's very expensive, and only a tiny minority of local people would be able to afford to use it.

In the evening I climbed to the highest point around, maybe 2,000 feet above the Camp, and suddenly found I had service on my phone. I phoned home and Brenda answered! It was lovely to talk to her (me shouting above the wind), and very surreal doing so on a mobile phone whilst surrounded by 2,000 metre peaks in the heart of Outer Mongolia.

June 27

I took a special English class with two of the naughtier boys, and they wrote, and then drew for me. Afterwards we played animal snap with 4 or 5 of the kids, and this has proved very popular. It's quite good, as I can ask them about the animals, and try to get them to describe them and where they come from etc. I also played draughts with two or three of the boys, and was easily beaten by all of them! Some of the children have very agile minds.

I'm pretty excited today, as tomorrow it's back to UB for a shower and a shave, and to meet some of the other volunteers who are working there.

June 28

The jeep to take me back was about four hours late, as usual, but I arrived in UB, at about 4pm. After showering etc, I met Del, and we went to Tseren Travel, and fixed up what has now expanded to a six day trip to the Gobi, leaving on July 25. There will be a huge amount to see, and we are both really looking forward to it. Later we went to Dave's Place for the Thursday Quiz (Dave's is a real slice of home for the expats). There were about eleven tables, all outside overlooking the main square, and our group of Projects Abroad volunteers came fourth. Could've been worse...

June 29

Drifted around town sending emails etc and got my clothes washed. Had lunch at Didi's vegetarian cafe, and again met Bratatii. She told me some stories about corruption in Mongolia. The worst was that of a volunteer at the Lotus Centre, who (while Didi was away) had sold a baby in the Centre for adoption in Russia, and had bribed the authorities to push through the adoption papers before Didi got back. Unbelievably the same woman applied for a posting the following year! Didi had made sure all the other orphanages knew the story, so she didn't get a position anywhere. She also told me that the hotel in which Ivan and I were supposed to be staying leans, and was originally refused an operating licence. Money changed hands, and now it is open. As it happens, Ivan's travel agent has changed the hotel, and we are now staying somewhere else, which may not be a bad thing!

I mentioned before that there had been a bad helicopter crash in the west, and there was a candlelight vigil in the main square in the evening to commemorate the dead. It was very moving.

I go back to Camp this afternoon, so will be in touch again in about 8 days…

June 30

Yes, it's Sunday morning, and I'm still here. The reason is that the American guy (Ramsay) who is working with a nomad family down the valley from the Summer Camp was supposed to be going back to Terelj with me yesterday, but got completely plastered the previous night. He was found sometime after midnight wandering about outside the Guest House, was persuaded to come in by the owner, but then went out again at 1 a.m. and was not seen again until yesterday evening! Projects Abroad were very concerned about him, and so we hung around until he reappeared. By then it was too late to go back to the Camp yesterday. I was a bit disappointed, as the kids were expecting me on Saturday, and I feel I've slightly let them down, but I guess it'll be okay. Alcohol abuse is a big problem amongst the local population. You see a lot of people begging who have missing fingers/hands/toes etc, and I assumed at first that they were suffering from leprosy. But apparently what happens is they get blind drunk, collapse in the street, and in the winter they are frostbitten overnight, gangrene sets in, and they have to have the affected area amputated.

The only thing interesting that happened yesterday is that two dishevelled looking guys on big Beamers rode into the main square with a police escort. I strolled down to find out who they were, and it turned out they were two Austrian bikers riding from Austria to New York "*The Long Way Round*", having been inspired by Ewan McGregor and Charlie Boorman. However, unlike Ewan and Charlie they did it without any back-up, and that's pretty impressive. I had quite a long chat to them, but didn't have my camera with me, so couldn't take any photos.

More when I return …

4 – THE THIRD SPELL IN SUMMER CAMP

Here I am back in UB for an extended break, as it is the Naadam Festival this week, and I am staying with Ivan for three nights, with another four nights in total in the Guest House. So to bring you up to date:

July 1

Finally arrived back in Camp after Ramsay's alcoholic episode. The girls in the Camp had spent the day making fashion clothes from stuff they found in and around the Camp. To me there is little but rubbish there, but with help from the ger mothers they produced some wonderful colourful clothes – sometimes I am astonished by their imagination and creativity. Didi and Bratatii arrived in the evening, and the kids modelled their clothes on a "catwalk" we made out of spare canvass. Unfortunately the battery on my camera was close to death, so I was only able to take photos on my old 35mm camera, but they should come out okay. Didi asked me if I would be a trustee of a charitable trust which she is proposing to set up as a fund raising vehicle, and I am feeling very honoured to be asked, as she has only known me for such a short time. At the moment she lives very much hand to mouth, existing almost exclusively on irregular private donations. She has to feed and clothe about 170 children, and pay the wages of the ger mothers, cook, teachers in the primary school, and all the other staff. She is concerned that if she ran out of cash then she simply would not be able to support the children, and many of them would either drift on to the street, or go back to parents who may have already physically or sexually abused them. She has a meeting at the beginning of October with the representatives of some very wealthy people, and she believes it would be easier to persuade them to make regular donations if she had a charitable trust to put the money into, rather than into her own bank accounts where it goes now. She is a remarkable woman, and I will do all that I can to help her.

Halfway through the evening gentle Galaa suddenly went wild. I'd never seen him like that before, but something that the oldest of the special needs girls said or did really upset him. He was ranting and raving, and picking up large stones, and threatening to hurl them at anyone who came within range. Some of the other children were frightened, and the ger mothers didn't really know how to cope as, physically, he is an adult. After a bit of a struggle I was able to get hold of him and cuddle him, and eventually he subsided and broke down and sobbed. I felt desperately sorry for him.

In the evening I met Chimgee, who has joined the Camp for a few days. She teaches outdoor survival skills and personal development.

July 2

Chimgee took me and four of the ger mothers on an all day trek to a monastery deep in the Terelj. Someone said it was 30 kilometres, but the Mongolian idea of distance is about as good as their idea of time, and I am sure it was less then that. But it was up and down the hills, and there are no paths, so it was quite hard going. It was very hot in the morning, so I wore shorts and a tee shirt, with my hat and lots of sun-cream. I took just water and dried fruit with me. Just after mid-day a thunderstorm broke, the temperature fell dramatically, and I was soaked through and cold – serves me right for going out ill-prepared. One of the girls gave me a thin shirt to wear on top of my tee-shirt, but as she is tiny (they mostly are) it hardy stretched across my back, let alone buttoned up!

When we got back in the evening, Osko (a teacher of about my age (ancient!)) had been given some sort of state award (a bit like the MBE) for services to teaching and dance. I was told that one of the older boys at Lotus, Gantaluk, was particularly difficult when he arrived, and she had started teaching him traditional Mongolian dance last Autumn. He showed great natural ability and in April of this year he had gone to Japan with a local dance troupe. His behaviour has improved dramatically, and he is now one of the nicest children in the Camp. Mongolian dance is considered a very manly pastime, and some of the younger boys (noticeably some of the "tougher" ones) are now copying him as he practices, and are themselves showing real talent, and modified behaviour. It is "cool" to dance, and they are not in the least bit self-conscious about it.

There was a party for Osko in the evening, and she wore traditional clothes, and her medal. Two of her children had come and brought huge creamy cakes, plus biscuits and sweets, and we all indulged greedily. Zorig played his guitar, and sung by candlelight. Some of the ger mothers joined in, plus Enkhee who was educated partly in Russia, and who sang some traditional Russian songs – one of them being the tune immortalised in the west by Kenny Ball as "Midnight in Moscow" in the sixties! Anyone else remember that? The singing was hauntingly beautiful. It is not something I will forget easily. Zorig's contract ends in mid-July, but he has promised to come back for one night to sing to us when Brenda is here. He has little money, and this will cost him some work, but they have a generosity of spirit from which we all could learn. I was asked to contribute a song, and I sung "We Shall Overcome", having explained its origins in the black Civil Rights movement in America. My singing is pretty awful, but with Zorig accompanying me I guess it was okay – at least they applauded enthusiastically!

July 3

The weather in the valley is getting hotter by the day. It was 35 when we drove down three days ago, and today started out a scorcher. The problem is that this has awoken the insect population with a vengeance, and a significant proportion of them seem to have decided that my ger, with its warmth, its easy access through the many holes in the floor and the walls, and its inherent filth, is the home they have always dreamed of. At times it appears to be teeming with the local wildlife – and sometime this morning I spotted Mr Big of the insect world scuttling across the floor. I don't know why he was bothering to scuttle so fast, as he was far too big for me not to see. The splat he made when introduced to my right walking boot must have been two inches wide. I then had to secretly remove the body as it is a serious offence in the Summer Camp to destroy any living creature! I guess the concept complements the vegetarian diet. So I felt like a character out of Pulp Fiction as I hid the remains in my toilet paper and made a trip to The Pit.

As a result of this episode I have erected a series of defences to protect my sleeping bag from invaders during the day. First I zip it up to its full extent, then I roll it, then I cover it with blankets. We shall see how successful this is. The good news is that when Brenda comes I have been promised that I will move to the teaching ger, which is immaculate by comparison, and almost brand new. The bad news is that this is still six weeks away, and hey – why should she get special treatment? What's good enough for me...

In the afternoon we had a spectacular storm. Choking dust first, followed by thunder and lightning and driving rain. We were confined to our gers, and I spent the time draping an aerial around the inside walls of my ger, and up and across the roof. As a result, when I went to bed that night I was finally able to locate the BBC World Service on my short wave radio. I lay there in the dark at 10pm (3pm London time) listening to the news, followed by live rain falling at Wimbledon. It was wonderful to hear that Alan Johnston had been released after four months of captivity. Let us now hope that we respond by recognising Hamas – after all they are the elected body, at least in Gaza.

July 4

I woke up this morning, to find that the Mongol (Insect) Hordes had penetrated my carefully planned defences and I had seven or eight bites on my ankles and legs. They itch pretty badly, but I was comforted to learn that Zorig has also been bitten – so they are not discriminating solely against the fair skinned western visitor!

It is another really hot day, but I have learnt to prop up the skirt of my ger with sticks, which stops it getting too stuffy – otherwise it is unbearable by mid-day. This is the last day that Chimgee will be here, and I had a long chat with her in the afternoon. She comes from a difficult background – her father drank a lot (a recurring theme here) and used to beat her mother. They divorced when Chimgee was seven, but although brought up very simply in the country she managed to get a place at the university. She then married, had three children, divorced, and did a masters degree in her spare time. The academic standards are not the same as in the west, but this was still a real achievement. She then received a scholarship to go to Singapore on an Outward Bound training course, and now teaches "moral education" plus outward bound and survival skills, and personal development. She is self employed, and clearly finds life tough. Her sister has a heart problem, and no husband, and her mother is elderly. So on what Chimgee can earn she has to keep herself and her three children, her sister and her two children, and her mother. She would like to work as a teaching assistant in the west, maybe in a special needs school, but although she has made applications to England and Australia, and was once shortlisted, to date she has had no luck. At first I wasn't sure what she had to offer to the Camp, but I have grown to like her, and she will be missed.

Didi came in the evening and brought back a child who had been to the dentist. There are 2 or 3 children here who have big round circles of toothpaste on their cheeks. They have toothache, and they think this will relieve it! Didi has tried explaining that it will not help, but the ger mothers don't listen.

Chimgee told me that there had been an incident earlier in the day with the older girl who had successfully wound up Galaa.

She believed she had been promised she would be going to an activity camp for special needs adults, but this had been cancelled. She thought Didi had let her down and was very angry. She was shouting that all foreigners were liars, and was carrying a large rock, saying that she was going to "*kill Fraser*" – presumably because I was the only foreigner around at the time! Zorig and Osko contained her, and then Didi spoke to her in the evening. I also spent some time with her, and she is calm now.

July 5

Two of the most likeable kids here are sisters, Inkhzaya and Inkhchumick aged about eight and five. They have big round faces, which light up when they smile – which is pretty well whenever they catch sight of me. They seem to be very carefree, although they had only just arrived at Lotus when I got here, so were still settling in. The little one wears a golf cap with the Ping logo, so I always call her "Ping". Didi told me yesterday that the police brought them to Lotus because Inkhzaya was being repeatedly raped by her stepfather. It is difficult for me to contemplate such barbarity, and impossible to understand it.

Didi revealed today that she has a cash problem. She pays VAT on everything she buys (no relief for an orphanage), but the taxman is now saying she should have been paying an extra 3% on all her purchases over the years. This amounts to a large sum, and she has also been told that if she doesn't pay it by the end of the week then they will confiscate all her bank accounts. The advice she has been given is that the authorities are wrong, but she cannot have her assets confiscated as that would mean she could not buy food, let alone pay the wages of her staff. So she has had to set aside the amount in question, and will pay this unless there is some last minute change. This is a major blow to her already fragile finances. She is an extraordinarily calm and resourceful person but even she is showing the strain now. Osko is trying to help, and we shall see what happens.

On a lighter note, I have run out of soft toilet paper, so am looking forward to fresh supplies arriving with Ivan. The alternative available in the Camp resembles industrial strength cardboard, and is liable to make corrugations across ones' backside similar to those perpetrated by the last Ice Age on the Alps!!

July 6

I am being taken back to UB today for a "Projects Abroad" dinner, and I am then staying on for a long break over Naadam. So I packed my stuff in the morning, and compared fresh bites with Zorig – he remains in the lead by a short head, and I generously donated to him some of my Aussie bite cream. I also have anti-histamine tablets if it gets too bad.

Had a really good English lesson this morning. My star pupil is Ariunzea, a very pretty girl of 12 who has come on in leaps and bounds since I arrived. This is a big help to me, as if there is anything complicated to say in the lesson I can tell Ariunzea, and she then translates it for me. We played Old Maid after the formal lesson, and they picked it up instantly – bright kids. I try to end the lesson with a card game or some other game, but insisting (they sometimes ignore me of course) that they try to speak only English when they are playing.

By the late afternoon, there is still no sign of my transport, and a mini crisis is looming in the Camp, as we have run out of the gas cylinders that are used for cooking. This means that the cook will have to try to produce three meals a day for 100 people using a makeshift wood fire outside. A good time for a break...

It's now 9.30pm, and still no car, so I am resigned to staying another night. I am dismantling my sleeping bag defences, when a chant from the kids of "*Didi comes*" spreads through the Camp! We all race outside, and sure enough there is Didi in her battered vehicle, bearing not only Del, to stay the night, but also an enormous bag for me which she had collected from Ivan, who had arrived in UB that day. This was revealed to contain not only teaching equipment, but also tee-shirts, underwear, football shirts, shorts and skirts for the children. Much of the clothing was organised and paid for by friends in the office, and the rest had been acquired by Brenda. The clothes have arrived with perfect timing, as some of the children are going to a concert of song and dance in Terelj village on Saturday, and will be able to wear their new clothes. Enkhee is delighted.

July 7

The vehicle to take me (and Del now) back to UB finally arrived about 11.30. The kids have been given their brand new reversible football shirts (blue on one side, red on the other), and a game is in full swing as we prepare to leave. They all know that I am going to be away for a few days, and many of the children gather round for cuddles and waves as I go. It brings a lump to the throat. There will be many tears (from all of us) when I finally go for good.

July 8

Back in UB and after the delicious ritual shower and shave, I took the bus out to the orphanage to see how the little ones were doing. I hadn't been back since my first day at the Camp a month ago. At that time a baby of about four months was a recent arrival, suffering from syphilis. She appeared to be blind, showing no reaction at all when anything was passed across in front of her eyes. She is gorgeous, and I went to see her first. I bent over her cot, smiled, and she beamed back at me! Her sight is recovered! Wonderful news – and another "lump in throat" moment. She is clearly behind, but seems normal, and now has a real opportunity in life.

The Chinggis Guest House, where I normally stay, is full, but the owner knows me well now, and has put me in an apartment just down the road, occupied apart from me just by a Canadian VSO volunteer, and his girl friend who has arrived for a couple of weeks' holiday. My room is huge – a queen sized bed, plus two single beds! There is also a good sized kitchen, and a toilet and separate bathroom which we share. Pure luxury at 10 pounds a night!

Went with most of the other volunteers to a Karaoke club in the evening. Not really my scene, but after two large Chinggis beers (everything here is named after the Great Man), I managed a stunningly bad version of "Summer of '69". Not a highlight …

5 – NAADAM

July 9 –July 14

The annual Naadam Festival is held in mid-July, and Ivan and I went for two days. Primarily it is intended as a celebration of the three "manly sports" of wrestling, horse racing, and archery. Did anyone know that the reigning Sumo world champion is a Mongolian? The stadium is about a couple of miles outside UB, and we walked out. I guess it holds about 10,000 people, and was packed for the opening ceremony. This comprised parades of dancers, riders in traditional costume (still worn by the nomads in Terelj where I work), and colourful floats. We then had a brief gig from Mongolia's leading rock singers, followed by a parade of big engined motor bikes (don't ask me why, as I have no idea...). The whole thing was a very strange mixture of the ancient and the modern. The most incongruous moment was when the traditional throat singers from the Gobi were drowned out by the roar of the Harley's as they rode off. It being Mongolia, of course not everything went to plan, and one of the bikes broke down and had to be pushed out of the stadium! But the dancing in particular was lovely, and all the participants clearly enjoyed themselves, and constantly smiled and waved to the crowd.

I've got to say that the wrestling is a bit dull. The object is to make your opponent touch the ground with any part of his body other than his feet or hands. There is a lot of slow-paced tactical manoeuvring, and bouts can go on for quite some time. You can wait 20 minutes for a bit of action, and then it is all over in a sudden burst of activity.

In the afternoon we went about 20 kilometres out onto the Steppe for the horse racing. I was told we were seeing the five year olds, and I assumed this would be the horses. Wrong – it was the riders who were five years old! The race we saw was over a straight course 30 kilometres long, and about 300 riders took part. We could see the dust miles away in the distance as they approached. The first few past us were all in good shape, and there was a dramatic sprint for the line. The skill of the children is astonishing – about half were riding bareback, and of course none had any form of riding helmet. We only saw one come off. However, sadly, I am told that over the two days of racing many horses die. I was talking to a Kiwi vet this morning, who was trying to help them, but the police would not allow him on the track until a horse went down, and by then it was usually too late. But I suppose we should not be judging such an ancient tradition by western standards.

Back at the stadium for day two we watched part of the archery (the women competitors wearing the traditional Del accompanied by high heels!), and wandered around the stalls – it is a bit like a country fair at home, with stuff for sale (not all of it made in China...) and various games. I tried knocking down the empty paint cans with three throws of something like a bean-bag, but missed twice. They all grinned and chattered away to me, delighted that I had had a go, and mildly amused by my incompetence.

For me the most interesting event was the 'ankle bone throwing'. This involves two sheeps' ankle bones placed in front of a box, and two teams taking alternate shots at hitting them from a distance of about four metres with a piece of polished stone, which they flick with their thumb or middle finger off a short polished wooden ramp. Each competitor warms up by flexing and blowing on his fingers, and then his own team encourages him with collective throat singing which starts quietly, and then builds to a crescendo as the "flicker" finally shoots. If he hits (as he frequently does) there is an explosion of deep throated noise from his team mates, and then they pass the stone back to him by tossing it high in the air through the hands of each of them until it gets back to the flicker – a bit like a fielding team in cricket passing the ball back to a fast bowler via the wicket keeper, slips, and mid-off.

In the evening back in UB there was the finest firework display I have ever seen – it must have gone on for at least 20 minutes as we watched from the terrace at Dave's Place. Hugely impressive for all the tourists now in town, but is this money well spent for such a poor nation? Still – we had fun.

After the next day I said goodbye to Ivan, whom I have really enjoyed having here, and met Del and Hanson at Ananda (Didi's veggie café) for lunch. The food there is excellent and terrific value – pasta, freshly squeezed apple juice, and a muffin afterwards, for three dollars. But today's lunch was made particularly interesting as two policemen got into a fight with each other right outside the door! They ripped open their tunics, and really laid into one another – one of them had blood pouring from his nose and mouth, and running down his tunic and vest. While this was going on a drunk was happily urinating against a tree just alongside them! The fight stopped when the drunk decided to try to push the officers around, and the guy with his tunic open and blood all over his vest promptly arrested him. The really odd thing, and which shows how accustomed I have become to a completely different world, is that I found none of this particularly surprising. In just six or seven weeks I have become a part of a totally different society.

I have two more days off, and tomorrow five of us are going to see the Mongolian wild horses (the Takhi) which are now preserved in a protected area about 100 kilometres south of the City. They are the only genuine wild horses in the world, having two chromosomes more (or is it less?) than the domestic horse. I am hoping for some good pictures. Speaking of which, I have now been able to recharge my camera battery, and will make another attempt as soon as I can to upload some photos.

When I get back from the horses I go straight to Camp, and I must say I miss the kids, so it will be good to be with them again.

July 15

The Takhi are preserved in Khustain National Park, and are the most recognised symbol of the preservation and protection of Mongolia's unique wildlife. They are the forerunners of the domestic horse, as depicted in early cave paintings in France. By 1990 they were virtually extinct, after poachers killed them for meat, and overgrazing and human encroachment reduced their fodder and breeding grounds. At that time there were only a dozen left alive.

However, between 1992 and 2004, with assistance from international environmental agencies, the Takhi were carefully nurtured at Khustain, and also at Takhiin Tal, in the north west of Mongolia. Today there are about 150 Takhi in Khustain, and 60 in Takhiin Tal – all descended from the bloodline of three stallions. Computerised records have been introduced to avoid in-breeding.

We arrived at Khustain in the early evening after a long drive along rough tracks. We had rented two gers in a small tourist encampment on the edge of the Park, which were equipped with comfortable beds and stoves that had been lit just before we arrived. Rather more comfortable than the children's summer camp in Terelj!

In addition to the wild horses, Khustain contains populations of Maral (Asiatic red deer), steppe gazelle, wild boar, wolf, lynx, and marmot.

We had arranged for our driver to wake us at 5.30 a.m., as we had been told that the best time to see the Takhi is in the early morning. We drove for about 45 minutes before the driver suddenly stopped and pointed. Not less than 100 metres away there was a group of four mares, a stallion, and three foals, grazing by a stream. We walked carefully towards them, and were able to crouch down not more than 20/30 metres away and watch them, on our own, for at least half an hour. It was a beautiful sight. Afterwards we drove across the steppe and stopped in a nomad encampment where we were treated to cups of Airag (fermented mare's milk) and Aaruul, which are dried milk curds. They were as hard as a rock, and about as tasty!

The driver dropped us off about five kilometres from the ger encampment so that we could walk back. There was complete silence as we walked, and we were lucky enough to see both wild deer and marmot – although we stayed well clear of the latter as they still carry the bubonic plague, of which there are a number of cases in Mongolia every year.

Back in the encampment we had an excellent dinner in a wooden building adjoining the gers, and then sat and chatted by the light of our fires until late. Ed, a Canadian medic, showed me an extraordinary photo of a Mongolian surgeon in the middle of an operation working away with his scalpel, whilst at the same time chatting on his mobile phone tucked between his shoulder and his chin! Remind me not to get sick here....

We were brought back to UB by jeep in the early morning. It had been a fascinating experience.

6 – THE FOURTH SPELL IN SUMMER CAMP

July 16

After a whole week away I was happy to get back to the Camp, and received an overwhelming, emotional and humbling welcome from the children. They seem really to love me, and what little can I offer them in just eleven weeks?

In my absence there have been snakes in the Camp! One was found in Enkhee's ger, and there have been several others spotted in and around the area. Enkhee was unsure whether they are poisonous or not, but said she had been frightened. To protect me, the children have sprinkled ash from the fires in the Camp round the outside of my ger. I hope that this does the trick!

I had brought back some sausage and bread with me from UB, and the ger mothers, Enkhee and Zorig retreated to my ger to consume it with the door firmly shut, so that nobody else knew we were eating meat! I was really pleased to find Zorig still here, as he was expecting to leave the Camp after Naadam, but his contract has been renewed until at least the end of July. He speaks not a word of English, and I still have only about 30 words of Mongolian, but we are great mates.

In the late afternoon we played football on a pitch, complete with goalposts, which has been constructed in my absence by the boys. Zorig played on one side, and me on the other. I scored (amazingly) with a volley from my own half! It was 3-3 at full time, and we won with a golden goal in extra time.

Two children have been appointed "Camp Captains" – Chinzorig (who thrashed me at draughts, and scored the golden goal in the footie) is the boy's captain, and Ariunzea is the girl's captain. They are both lovely, talented, kids. Their job is to make sure the Camp is clean and tidy, to stop any bullying or fighting (there is very little of either), and generally to help with the smooth running of the

Camp. They are both only 12 or 13, but are remarkably mature and sensible, and I am certain will do well when they finally leave Lotus and move on in life.

July 17

"*I have a problem with my anus!*" Not the sort of thing that I would expect the camp manager to announce, but this is what Enkhee had said to me on the day before I last left the Camp. After some complicated explanation in "Monglish" I deduced this to mean haemorrhoids. I've had the problem myself in the past when trekking over long distances, and I keep some suitable suppositories in my medical kit. I gave a couple to Enkhee, miming how she should use them, fearful that she might think that they are an oral remedy. I am pleased now to hear on my return that she is feeling a lot better. On the subject of mime, and sticking to the same orifice, Del had a serious squits problem last week, and went to the chemist to get some help. The chemist spoke no English at all, so Del mimed the problem in all its gory detail to the delight of the other customers. To make sure she had understood, the chemist mimed the problem back to him, and satisfied that they were on the same wavelength, she duly dispensed the local version of Imodium.

Enkhee also announced today that this is English week, and each of the gers will be expected to learn and perform a song, a poem, and "maybe some drama" in English, by Saturday. I am also expected to arrange some sort of English competition! I explained that I knew no suitable songs, had no poetry with me, and how was I supposed to teach eight separate groups of children "some drama" in four days? All of this fell on deaf ears. We shall see what happens. Sometimes I am told this sort of thing, and then it all just gets forgotten about. Anyway, in the afternoon I rummaged around in the books I have with me, and found and adapted some short poems. At least I have made a start.

In the evening, Osko returned from a visit to UB bringing with her a huge packet of mini doughnuts and some fruit tea. I over-indulged in both in the ger that she shares with Zorig, and went to bed happy.

July 18

The weather has changed. The great heat and sudden storms of June and early July have gone, and it is now cooler – maybe 20/22 degrees. Enkhee tells me that trees start to change colour as early as August, and by the end of August Autumn is here. By late September there can be snow on the ground. When I remember that the day I got here it was 1 degree, it shows what a short summer they have.

Two specialist dance teachers have arrived in the Camp, and are staying for three days to prepare the children for a show. They are working them really hard – some of them are doing up to seven hours practice a day, starting before breakfast. Would you get Western kids aged between 8 and 14 to do that?

Galaa has a headache, and has been calling for his mum. He has been at Lotus for five years, having been rescued from a dreadful institution for special needs and mentally ill adults. I am told that the conditions were not much different from Bedlem 150 years ago. When he arrived at Lotus he had no name. They do not know how long he was in the hospital, but he can remember snatches of his earlier life. He sometimes speaks of his brothers and sisters, and talks of his dad driving a car. Nobody knows now who or where they are. This place is full of heartbreaking stories. He told me that he would buy a Microbus when he grows up, and drive it round Mongolia with me as his passenger. I gave him some Neurofen.

July 19

Chinzorig is the most talented boy in the Camp. He is the best footballer, draws beautiful pictures with no effort at all, speaks good English, and is academically very bright. His mother is a bag lady in UB, and he is believed to have six brothers and sisters. Nobody knows who his dad is. His mum used to take him and his younger brother on the buses in the winter, to keep warm (it can be minus 40°C in January). He had a habit of spitting on the other passengers as they climbed the steps to get on, and Didi met him when he scored a direct hit in her face one morning! Gradually Didi got to know him and his mum, and one day his mum just turned up at the orphanage and left him there. I guess she recognised that he stood a better chance there than with her, and made the sacrifice to try to give him a future. If she knows how well he is doing know, and what a nice lad he is, she would be proud of him. He is the only child in the orphanage who goes to a private school (although Ariunzea will be following him in September), and when he first went there he deliberately got things wrong, so that he would not stand out. He's got over that now, and his ambition is to get into university, do a masters overseas, and then come back to Mongolia to use his education here. I am sure he has the ability to achieve that ambition.

In the morning Nyamaa and I took eight of the older kids (including Chinzorig) on a long hike to look for wild strawberries which were apparently to be found in another part of Terelj. We walked for hours, but found nothing. The only consolation for the older boys was that they came across three young local girls, and chatted to and wandered with them for a while. Eventually we gave up the search, and trailed back into Camp after eight hours to an expectant welcome, only to have to confess that we had no fruit with us! We had run out of water on the way back, but in Mongolia that is no problem – we just stopped at a couple of nomad gers, and picked up some on the way. Remember that water is a precious commodity, but they had no hesitation in sharing what they had. It is one of the lessons I will try to take home from here. In the absence of any fresh fruit, I shared out most of my remaining dried fruit, and that at least was appreciated by my tired fellow walkers.

Chatting afterwards with Chinzorig, I was teasing him about the three girls he had met. He suddenly pointed at the Camp entrance, and said "*Fraser … Brenda*." I spun round to look, and of course there was nobody there. I turned back, and he burst out laughing. I'll get him back …

A maths teacher from Sydney, Anne, has arrived in Camp for five days, and I am looking forward to working with her. It will be much easier with two of us teaching together.

July 20

When I got back from yesterday's walk there was a message that the Projects Abroad people were going to collect me today to go to Kharkhorin, the ancient capital of Mongolia in Chinngis' time. But it's a two day trip, and the kids had been preparing with the dance teachers and Zorig for a concert today, so I decided not to go. To me it was more important to be in the Camp. I was right – the concert was magical. Once again I was captivated by the remarkable talent possessed by many of the children. The singing was lovely, but it was the dancing which caught the eye. They had only three days to practice, but they had been working incredibly hard to learn and perfect the dances. I cannot see western school children prepared to give that level of commitment during their summer break. It was a privilege to be there and watch the flowering of such ability from children whose backgrounds could not, in most cases, be more disadvantaged. Before the concert began Enkhee had announced that it was especially for me and Anne, the overseas visitors. I was deeply moved by the whole event, and had to pinch myself to remember that I was in the heart of this wild and beautiful country, watching abused and orphaned children perform so beautifully for my benefit. I wept.

Despite all this immersion in Mongolian culture, I am still making minimal progress with the language. If you can imagine two cats spitting and snarling at each other, and then one throws up, that's what a conversation sounds like! Still, I will continue to persevere...

In the evening, the last of the dance teachers' visit, Anne and I were invited after "lights out" to join the teachers, Enkhee, and Zorig, in Osko's ger. There she produced a huge box of chocolates and some more illicit sausage and bread. However, best of all, and with a sly smile, Zorig suddenly drew out from his bedding a bottle of Bulgarian wine! We had no corkscrew, but after much effort (and to cheers from the assembled company) I was able to ram the cork into the bottle with a metal spike, and we consumed it greedily.

A perfect day ended with my lying in my ger listening to Test Match Special on the World Service!

July 21

Anne teaches maths teachers in Oz, and has 35 years teaching experience. It is so much easier working as a team, particularly when one of you knows what she is doing! She is here until July 24, and has brought with her some number games so that the children are doing maths without realising it. This has been a great success, and as we do all the classes in English (well, we have no choice, really), they are learning maths and English at the same time. Together we taught for a total of four hours today, and it proved very rewarding (much more so than the law...)

In the early evening the boys borrowed the football kit again – and Chinzorig ensures that it is returned to my ger each time it is used, so that it doesn't get lost. I also gave him today a beginner's guide to chess, designed for children (in English) which he will read over the next couple of days, and then I will try to teach him the game.

Just as the Camp was going to bed, Enkhee told me that tomorrow would be the planned English day – songs, poems, and "maybe some drama!" Because of the focus on the concert I have done no preparation at all – gulp! I went to bed wondering what on earth I was going to do...

July 22

Just when you think a child is perfectly adjusted, something happens to remind you that all these children come from very difficult backgrounds which leave them with deeply ingrained issues. Today is English day, and I had just about no idea what I was going to do, apart from the English competition that Enkhee had asked me to organise, of which more in a minute.

I was more concerned about the singing and poetry – I had been told that there would be eight teams, and that I would be asked to judge the first three places. Was I supposed to have prepared something for each of them? It was not at all clear to me, and the language barrier was badly letting down both me and Enkhee. However, each of the teams had been practising their pieces with their ger mothers, and without my help. What a relief! All I had to do was listen, and award marks. The singing was very good (simple English songs such as "Twinkle Twinkle Little Star"); the poetry less recognisable! I think it would have been better if I had been involved in the preparation, but it was fun. I had three teams all tying for first place, and they each were awarded prizes.

For the English competition, I used the flash cards that my daughter Sarah had sent down with Ivan. The participants lined up in front of me, I showed them the picture side, and they had to say the word in English. I had graded the cards so that they got progressively more difficult. They were asked to identify cards in turn, and a child who made three mistakes was out of the competition. Chinzorig had elected not to take part, presumably thinking it would be too easy for him, or a bit of a bore. But he hung around, making a nuisance of himself by whispering the answers. Then, after we had gone several rounds of the children, he decided he would like to take part after all (like a high jumper electing to join in the third round in the Olympics!). Enkhee (quite rightly) told him it was too late to change his mind, and he then became a bit more disruptive, by deliberately prompting the others to give wrong answers. I found a yellow card and showed it to him light-heartedly in the hope that it would defuse things, but he went on being a nuisance. Finally, exasperated, Enkhee sent him to his ger. It was then that he lost it, picking up a stone, flinging it in the direction of Osko, and hitting her on the ankle. She was quite badly hurt, and had to lie in her ger for the rest of the day watching it swell up. I gave her some pain-killers. Chinzorig disappeared to his ger.

For the record, Ariunzea won the competition, and I gave her a white Adidas baseball cap with an England badge on it, with which she was delighted, and which she has been wearing ever since.

We left Chinzorig alone, which was probably the best thing to do, and before the end of the day he had gone over to Osko's ger and apologised to her. He is a good kid, and I like him very much.

In the afternoon, and continuing the English theme, Anne and I organised some western type games – a three legged race; a game in teams passing a football between the legs down the line of the team; and a "ping pong ball and spoon race".

In the evening, now feeling a bit better, Osko went back to UB to attend some meetings to try to resolve Didi's tax problem, which is still dragging on.

July 23

Del arrived with Didi in the morning to stay overnight, together with a Canadian ex-teacher by the name of Sarah, who will be staying for two weeks. This is good news, as Anne will be leaving tomorrow, but there will be still be two of us to teach together. Best of all, Umesh came down with them for the day, and it was really good to see him again. I read with him for a while, and gave him a spare set of the football kit, with which he was delighted. I think I mentioned before that he can't stay in the Camp as he has bad epileptic fits.

Both Ankhar and another older boy have been missing from the Camp for a couple of days. This happens from time to time – maybe they go back for some medical treatment, or maybe for some specialist tuition. I asked Enkhee about them. Apparently the older boy was sent back to the orphanage because he sexually assaulted one of the girls. She didn't tell me the details. In Ankhar's case, he had climbed over the roof of, and into, the cooking ger, overnight, and stolen some food. I knew nothing of any of this, and I was very disappointed for Ankhar – it didn't seem to me to be a particularly serious offence (in fact I thought it showed some ingenuity!), and I suspect they took the opportunity to send him back because he is not well liked. They are not good in the Camp in dealing with any kids who are at all disruptive (and in particular the special needs children), as I found out later in the day. What they need is counsellors to assist them. I know that Didi is trying to hire someone, but as usual money is the problem. Del had seen Ankhar in the orphanage the previous day, and he had asked if I would be coming to see him. I will certainly do so when Brenda is here.

The early evening was disrupted by a visit from the wives of two Japanese politicians. They distributed sweets, crisps and chaos, took their photos, and then departed in their gleaming four-wheel drives. The kids were left as high as kites, and we spent the rest of the evening bringing them down, and picking up sweet papers. But I am sure the photos will go down well back home. Politicians are the same the world over.

Just before bedtime Sarah, Del, Anne and I had a real problem with one of the girls, Hongra, who is about 10, and has recently described her rape to Nyamaa, with whom she has a really good relationship. She would not leave Sarah's ger, which cannot be locked. It was bedtime, but the more we took her out, the more difficult and aggressive she became. Eventually I took her firmly by the hand, and led across the campsite to her ger, where I left her. A few minutes later I heard a bit of a commotion from the kids. The little girl was sitting outside the back of her ger punching herself, and scratching her face and legs. It was awful to see, and the other children were laughing at her. Fortunately Ariunzea came up, and I asked her to call Nyamaa. Less happily one of the other ger mothers arrived on the scene, and just shrugged her shoulders, and pointed to her head, as if to say that the child is a bit mad. As I said, they are not good with the special needs children. The episode left me feeling a bit low, and in need of some professional help with the children from someone with some real experience of dealing with their many problems.

Tomorrow I go back to UB for a shower and a change of clothes before meeting up with my friends the following day and travelling down to Gobi in an old Russian four wheel drive, accompanied by a driver and a guide.

7 – LETTER FROM THE GOBI

July 25 –July 29

I am writing this from Mandelgovi: a hot, dusty, ramshackle town in the northern part of the Gobi desert. We have been travelling for over four days, and it is only the second small settlement we have passed through. The group comprises me; Del; Prisca, a Dutch medic and Del's girlfriend; Kath and Sian, two trainee vets; and Ralf, a Dutch IT guy. I am told that the internet access in the town is sketchy, so if I just disappear, you will know that the connection has gone down.

The Gobi desert is one of the most remote and forbidding places on the planet. For vast areas it comprises nothing but stone, grit and sand. It is unforgivingly hot, and there is dust permanently in the wind. The horizons are huge – you seem to be able to see forever, and there is often absolutely no sign at all of human involvement. This is nature at its most brutal. For all that it has a fascinating beauty. And things do live there – we have seen wild Bactrian camels, wild goat with long horns (Ibex), and lizards and insects. Plus one very nasty looking snake – the guide told us that she had never seen a snake in the Gobi, but I had been told by Gek, a Singaporean volunteer at Lotus, that in the far south close to the Chinese border there is a particularly venomous snake that should be avoided at all costs, as the only anti-serum is kept in Beijing. So we gave this creature a very wide berth....

Despite the remoteness of the terrain, there are still nomads living around the fringes fighting for a living maintaining camels, and some goats, and occasionally a handful of sheep. These are tough people indeed. On the second day it was too hot and dusty to sit outside and eat our lunch, so we stopped at one of these gers, and were invited in with that wonderful hospitality that is so common in people who live the simple life all over the world. We were given dried yoghurt, cakes, and a soup containing small pieces of meat (I know not from which animal), and drank tea with the family. They are unhesitatingly and naturally generous.

There have been some surprises – the most dramatic being the long trek on day three deep into a remote canyon where the thin stream is covered in ice all the year round. An extraordinary sight, even though as each year goes by there is less and less ice to be seen. On the same day we had climbed high on a wonderful pass through the mountains that border the southern edges of the desert and discovered green hills and a cool breeze – it was a bit like Scotland, but 100 times as large! There are also occasional beautifully sculptured sand dunes which suddenly appear after hours of flat nothing, and these are a welcome relief.

We have tents with us, but every night bar one I have slept outside, falling asleep gazing at an enormous sky, and millions of stars. The exception was last night when shortly after we arrived in camp we saw a sandstorm approaching in the distance. It took about twenty minutes to arrive, in which time we stowed all our kit in the tents, and then sat inside waiting for it to hit. The wind arrived first, followed by squalls of rain, and then the sand and grit – it got everywhere, and I hate to think what it would be like to be caught outside in such a storm. As it was, it soon passed, and we were fine. But it made me again ask the question – why on earth do people choose to live in such a place?

When the storm had gone we gathered some dried goat dung and made a fire, and sat round until late at night drinking vodka and chatting. But the guide was expecting a second storm (which in fact did not happen), so on this occasion I chose discretion, and slept in the tent with Ralf.

We have one more night here, and then we return to UB. It has been a remarkable experience, and I have the greatest possible admiration for the few humans who choose to make their living in such a harsh environment.

July 30

I mentioned in my last message that I was writing from Mandelgovi, a remote town in the desert. This is the home town of our driver, Dawaa. He took us to his house and it turned out to be a three roomed dwelling where he lives with his parents, his brother and sister-in-law, and their baby. They welcomed us with what is becoming familiar Mongolian hospitality – we were given milky salted tea with sweets and biscuits to start with, followed by bowls of stew with meat, potatoes, carrots and cabbage. They could not do enough for us, and I am humbled by the generosity of the people we are meeting.

That evening we camped at a lovely site in an area of high rocks and canyons. Again we gathered dung and made a fire and consumed another bottle of vodka. However, during the day things had started to go wrong with the Russian vehicle we are using. There seems to have been an issue with the battery and the starting mechanism. If you have a mechanical problem in Mongolia which you cannot solve yourself, you simply wait for the next vehicle to come by (unfortunately the RAC do not quite stretch that far), and hope that they can assist. On the first occasion we waited three hours for the next car, which was able to help by driving to the nearest ger (30 minutes away) and coming back with a part which enabled Dawaa to patch things up. This is what they do here – nobody would dream of not helping.

This morning, the first thing to go wrong was that we had a flat tyre when we woke up – there must have been a slow puncture. No real problem here, as Dawaa just put on the spare. However, we had not driven half a mile when the starter issue raised its head again, and we drifted to a halt. This time we got help in about 30 minutes and were on the move again in an hour. But this was the day that nothing went right for Dawaa – in all we had three breakdowns and two more punctures! Having used the spare, he had to take off the tyres and patch them as best he could with bits of rubber and glue. All this was done with great good humour, and not once did he stop smiling – but we did add one word to our limited Mongolian vocabulary..."*shawa*", as muttered by Dawaa on the occasion of the third puncture, roughly translates as "*oh, shit!*"

Dawaa's great talent lies in his remarkable direction finding. The desert is criss-crossed with rough tracks – some of which just seem to peter out into nothing. There are no maps, and nothing to guide the driver but his own skill. We asked the guide how he found his way, and she told us that he "recognised the hills". To our eyes there were very few hills, and those that there were all looked the same! He is only a young man, but his knowledge of this vast inhospitable area is extraordinary.

We finally arrived back in UB at about 10pm, and I was shocked to look in the mirror and see how filthy I was – covered in a grey gritty dust. I have showered before writing this, and am now really tired. Tomorrow I will do some washing, and prepare to return to the Camp.

July 31

So when I got back here last night there seemed to be thousands of people just sitting around outside. I discovered why this morning – apparently there has been a heat wave, with temperatures up to 40 degrees, which is very rare in this part of the world (but don't worry – George W has told us there is no global warming problem...). I am concerned for the children, as they will have spent much of their time swimming, and if I'm not around there is nobody to insist they put on the sun cream. At one point in June several of them were quite badly burnt, but their skin has been much better recently, and I hope they haven't gone downhill again.

I like the Chinggis Guest House, as there are so many intriguing people passing through. There are a group of Poles here at the moment who have just arrived from Russia by train. They were held up for twelve hours on the border, and I think this is not unusual; there are some Dutch volunteers here, and they were held up for six hours on the same train (Brenda – don't expect anything to be done in a hurry when you get here. You just have to relax and wait. I have learnt that, and I never get stressed about anything in Mongolia). Two or three weeks ago there was a reporter from The Times (Sam Knight, I think) who was preparing a long piece about the painful transition from communism to capitalism, and who are the winners and losers. I expressed surprise that he was staying in the Guest House at seven dollars a night, and he explained that the article was his idea, not specifically sanctioned by the foreign editor, and therefore he was on a minimal budget. He's an interesting person, and I look forward to reading his article.

I am going back to the Camp this afternoon. The weather has changed dramatically, and it has been raining for the past two days. The streets are awash, but it is really pleasant to feel the moisture and the cool air after the heat of the Gobi. I have bought sausage, gherkins, bread, cakes and fruit juice to take back with me, and Zorig, Enkhee, Osko, Nyamaa, Oyuna (to whom I teach English each evening) and I will have a feast in my ger tonight! It is high time I returned their hospitality!

This will be my last long stint in the Camp, as Brenda arrives on 12 August, but she and I will go back for two days on 13 August. It will be fun this week, as we are taking the kids to a tourist camp for two days and one night. The ger mothers can't wait, as we will be eating in a restaurant, and there should be meat! I ran into one of the City based Lotus workers at Didi's vegetarian cafe at lunchtime today, and she told me that Osko had come into town to get her hair done so that she would look nice when I got back! Osko is about the same age as I am, but I am afraid she looks a lot older. The average Mongolian life span is very short compared to ours in the west. We tend to forget how lucky we are. I think the real point of the hair-do is so that I can take her photo! I am looking forward again to this visit, as I have been missing the children.

8 – FINAL DAYS IN THE CAMP

August 1

I arrived back in Camp to a wonderful, emotional welcome as the kids raced over for cuddles and high fives. Their affection is completely open and unreserved, which to me is remarkable, bearing in mind the scars that so many of them bear. They know that I shall be going soon, but just appear to accept it. Saying "goodbye" will be very hard for all of us.

I mentioned that they are going to a Tourist Camp tomorrow for two days, and they are incredibly excited. It is being paid for by a Mongolian IT company. They will be putting on a dancing display in the evening, and while I was in the Gobi they and the ger mothers have been designing and making costumes. They will look wonderful.

I had a chat to Nyamaa during the day, and she told me delightedly that she had got a teaching job in a state school. This will mean more money (US$200 a month) and the opportunity to improve her English (which is already quite good) so that she can work as a tourist guide in the summer. I am really pleased for her, as she has become a good friend.

In the evening most of the ger mothers joined me, Enkhee, Zorig and Osko (with her new hair-do!) in Osko's ger to consume the bread, sausage, pickles and fruit juice that I had brought down. The good news is that Osko and Zorig will both be giving up their spare time and staying on until 15 August, which will be my last day in the Camp. They and the children are all looking forward to meeting Brenda, and Enkhee confirmed that we will be given the new ger (I now have several mice enjoying my company in my ger!), for those two nights. Osko said that she would act as waitress and serve us food in the ger, and Zorig mimed that he would stand outside and keep away any small intruders, so as to ensure our privacy!

Didi (in the red hat)
with a group of Lotus children.

The play yard at The Lotus Centre.
The pit toilet is in the top right hand corner.

A little girl (clutching a sweet)
in the Lotus play area.

A group of children at Lotus.
Inkhchumick is third from the right.

Didi with one of "her" babies.

Lotus children fetching water for the Centre in the Yarmag shanty town.

The baby girl born blind with syphilis. This was the moment, just after she had recovered her sight, when she beamed back at me as I looked into her cot.

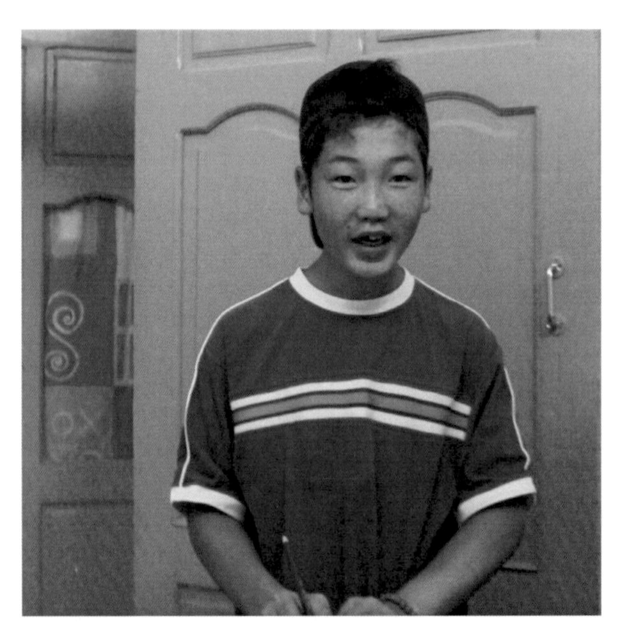

Umesh – my "shadow" when I first arrived at Lotus.

Children in the English class at the Lotus primary school. All of their school uniforms are handmade by their house mothers.

A little girl at Lotus. The photograph was taken just after her arrival. What stories do those sad eyes tell?

The Lotus Summer Camp viewed from a hill looking over the Terelj Valley.

The morning circle at the Summer Camp.

A storm gathering over the Summer Camp.

Ankhar.

Chinzorig.

Ariunzea in the cooking ger.

Uurganaa learning to read English in my ger.

Lotus children in their dancing costumes.

Gantaluk practicing dance with other boys.

Inkhzaya, who was raped by her stepfather.

Inkhchumick, Inkhzaya's younger sister.

The Author leaving Camp to go to Khustain.

The Naadam Parade.

Takhi – the Mongolian wild horse.

Rainbow on the Steppe.

Del meditating at Khustain.

The Author in the Gobi.

Bactrian camel in the Gobi – the flat, stony terrain is typical of the area.

Osko, Brenda, Ulie and Enkhee.

Osko.

Two street children rescued by Didi from the police.

Enkhee.

View of Ulaanbaatar from Zaisan Hill.

Chinzorig and Batra on the way to Erdenet.

Lotus children at Erdenet.
Ogoo is on the left, with the football.

Australian volunteer Ben playing with
children in the Lotus yard.

Zorig with the keyboard purchased by
Brenda's yoga classes.

Singing at the Camp opening ceremony 2008.

Bonfire at the Camp opening ceremony 2008.

The burnt out Communist Party headquarters
after the post-election riots.

I went to bed happy – although I miss my family very much, I am otherwise completely at home here. Can't say I miss Chancery Lane at all...

August 2

Never has the Camp been awake so early! The excitement of going to the Tourist Camp had all the children up and about before 7, whereas they are usually quiet until about 8! Everyone was packed and ready to go. And then we waited.....and waited.... and waited. By 11:30 there was still no sign of the bus. Then a call came through to Osko's mobile (she has a different service provider, and gets service in the Camp) to say that we would definitely be going, but maybe tomorrow. This is very Mongolian. "*Mar-gash*" means tomorrow, but it has the same connotations as "*mañana*" in Spanish. You just don't know when, or if, anything is going to happen. I have slipped quietly into this way of life, and don't get anxious about it. But it pervades the whole of their society, and in economic terms it cannot be good news. A relaxed life style is all very well, but they have a population to provide jobs for, and to feed, and if they are going to continue to expand their business relations with the West, then I think they will have to become more reliable.

We passed the time while we waited playing football, and drinking tea and consuming my last packet of chocolate biscuits in Osko's ger. Enkhee and some of the others put the finishing touches to the dancing costumes, which are quite beautiful. Finally, it was confirmed in the late afternoon that we would not be going to the Tourist Camp that day...mar-gash, maybe?

There is much apprehension in the Camp this evening as we have heard that there is a big storm coming. Apparently twenty gers have been destroyed in another district, and it is on its way here. We have been strengthening the ropes around our gers, and Zorig helped me tie a rope from the centre of the roof of my ger to the stove, and to weigh the stove down with stones. I shall let you know tomorrow if our defences were adequate...

August 3

The good news is that there was no storm (although secretly I am rather disappointed – it would have been exciting!). The bad news that we are not going to the Tourist Camp. The company that was donating the trip has deferred it to October. This is very unfair on the children, who were really excited about it. Once again someone has let them down. Absolutely nobody uses the Tourist Camps in October, when there is often already snow on the ground, so I guess it will cost the donor almost nothing then, which I assume is one reason for the postponement. What a shame.

Didi had returned the previous evening, and by way of some compensation she organised an early morning birthday ceremony for some of the children, catching up on those who had had birthdays over the last few weeks. Each of the birthday children had a present, and we sang "Happy Birthday" in Mongolian and English. We also had huge amounts of sickly birthday cake for breakfast (but that is a great improvement on the rice milk which we usually have, and which I don't mind if I never see again!). There was then a short dance presentation using the costumes that had been intended for the Tourist Camp. However, there are quite a lot of visitors due in August, so they will get plenty of use.

I learnt a bit more about Ankhar today. He was initially brought up with his mum in an adult psychiatric hospital until he was six. No wonder he craves attention, and no wonder he steals food. The conditions in those places are awful – apparently when Galaa arrived he was as thin as a rake, because you have to compete for the food. He looks fine now.

In the afternoon Ulie arrived – a German volunteer in her mid-thirties who is due to stay for three weeks. She seems really nice, and should fit in well. However, she went off again the same day for a three day visit to Kharkhorin, which I again turned down, so as to spend the time with the children. The Canadian girl, Sarah, has had to go home as her business partner is very ill, which is disappointing for her.

Just after Ulie had gone, a big four-wheel drive drew up to the Camp, and a wealthy looking Chinese guy got out and took a photograph of some of the children, who were doing dancing practice with Osko. It was hot, and the kids were in various states of undress, so I was not too impressed. However, I was still less impressed when he stepped over the fence, took out his light meter and long lenses, and started setting himself up! I strode over, put my hand over the lens, and told him in no uncertain terms to push off. He understood my coarse Anglo-Saxon message! It was the first time in Mongolia that I have really felt angry. I don't like to see the children treated as exhibits.

One of the girls cut herself badly while swimming. People just throw glass in the river, and this is the result. It is a nasty deep cut, but she made no fuss at all while Enkhee was dressing it. They are tough kids.

August 4

Galaa said he wants to come to England to live with me. He says it with a giggle, because he understands enough to know that he can't, but is just expressing his sadness that I will be gone in a couple of weeks.

Ariumbata is the least able of the special needs kids in the Camp. He was the one about whom Nyamaa said a few weeks ago..."*Perhaps he'll die*". I guess he is about 18, and he just wanders about the Camp all day doing nothing at all, except sometimes disrupting the other children. No attention is paid to him unless he does something wrong, and he lacks any form of stimulation. Even Didi says that he has no real quality of life. Apparently when he kicks off he can be quite violent, and is very strong – I am told that on one occasion he killed a cat by strangling it with his hands, and has been known to thrust his fist through a shop window to steal. However, I have seen none of that through the summer. I decided to spend a bit of time with him this morning. We went through some books together, with him looking at the pictures, and then he did some drawing. We shared some fruit. He was good and quiet the whole time. Obviously he needs some real attention and stimulation and then perhaps he would improve a bit. But there aren't the staff to do that, and the opportunities for children like him are very limited indeed. His future is about as bleak as it could be.

Another Australian friend of Didi (Tim) came to the Camp for a couple of hours. He told me he has been working with an ITN team investigating people trafficking in Mongolia. Young girls are taken and sold (principally to China) for prostitution. Most will not talk to the investigators, but a few have. One girl of about 21 has recently escaped back to Mongolia after three of her friends were killed and dumped in the river at Macau. Tim firmly believes that a high ranking official in the World Health Organisation is behind much of the trafficking, as his name crops up all the time, but as yet there is insufficient evidence to prove anything. We read about these things, but rarely do we get so close to the reality. It is truly horrific. I am learning a lot in a short space of time.

August 5

The oldest boy in the Camp (apart from Galaa and Ariumbata), has gone missing. He is 15. There has been no argument with any of the other children, but he didn't appear for dinner last night, and hasn't been seen since. The only clue is that he was complaining he didn't have enough clothes here, and we are hoping he may be making his way back to the Lotus Centre in UB. He could do this by walking to the road and then hitching a lift. Didi is here and is obviously worried about him. If he goes to the orphanage he will be fine, but if he just wanders about the city then he could be at risk, although he strikes me as being quite bright and resourceful. It leaves a bit of a shadow hanging over the Camp.

A group of Japanese tourists came by invitation, and the children dressed in their costumes, and sang and danced. The arrangement is that they come and make a donation. I am not sure I really like the kids being used as a tourist attraction in this way, but on the other hand the money is needed, and the children seem to enjoy showing off their talent. Also three friends of Didi came for the afternoon – two Dada's and a third person (Dada = brother; Didi = sister). They run a yoga and meditation centre in UB, having just arrived from Uganda, where they established a meditation centre and acupuncture clinic. They are very calm and relaxed people.

Zorig and Osko went to a party in a ger up the valley last night, and although Zorig was around first thing he has not been seen since. He may have had too much to drink, and made himself scarce as Didi is here. I think I mentioned before that he is said to have a drink problem.

Misha, an American/Japanese girl of 15 has arrived in the Camp for a week as a volunteer. Although she is very young she seems very sensible, and should be fine.

At dusk I usually go down to the river to sit quietly for a bit, and maybe write up my diary. On this occasion Galaa followed a few paces behind me, and then sat a few metres away as we watched the river. As I turned to walk back I saw he was crying. He attempted to hide it by pulling his baseball hat over his eyes, and then tried to dry them on his tee-shirt. I put my arm around him, and he sobbed quietly for a bit, before again drying his eyes and walking slowly with me back to the Camp. He is sad that I am leaving, and I will have been one more person just passing briefly through his life. Do we do the right thing, or would they be better off if we didn't come in the first place? And do we come for us, or for them? I don't know the answers.

There is no sign of the missing boy.

I just spent two hours typing five days, and lost the lot. So here goes again...

August 6

Didi is taking some of the older girls to UB for a few days to go to her yoga classes. Of course they all wanted to go, but there is limited capacity in her people carrier, so eventually she took about seven of them. She told me about one of the little girls whose mother is a prostitute. She came to Lotus when she was five, but a year later her mother took her back, only to "trade her" for a new ger. Some time after that her grandfather finally brought her back to the orphanage. How does a little girl cope with that kind of rejection?

Before they went I found Ariunzea in tears (which I had never seen before) wandering about just outside the Camp. I joined her and asked her what was wrong. After a while she simply said "*Chinzorig bad boy*". It seems that he had hit her, but when I asked him about it he said he had hardly touched her. I couldn't really get to the bottom of it. Nobody else in the Camp took any notice.

The atmosphere in the Camp is beginning to change. There is little enthusiasm for the English and maths classes, the children are becoming a bit bored, and Enkhee and the ger mothers are tired. Remember they have to care for, feed, organise, and entertain over 80 children of all ages all day every day; as well as treating their illnesses, dealing with their many cuts and bruises, washing their clothes and bedding, and resolving any disputes. At least ten of the children have special needs. Most of the staff have family or boy friends back in the city, and they have had less breaks than I. It is hard going, and I have the greatest respect for them. On 1st September the children will be back at school, and so they will start to send the kids back to the city in phases, starting in about a week's time.

In the afternoon, Enkhee and I and one of the ger mothers popped out to buy bread and matches – essential supplies of which we had run out. This involved a round trip of nearly four hours! On the way we were caught by a hail storm, and got soaking wet. But it was a lovely walk, through some stunning countryside.

August 7

There is still no news of the missing boy, but it seems that he spoke to the driver of a tourist bus, told him that he was fed up, and the driver gave him some money and his mobile number. This all appears rather sinister to me. The police have been informed.

This morning there was a series of competitions between the gers. They were given twenty minutes to write a poem on a given subject; they then had to draw a picture illustrating some socially unacceptable behaviour and its result (for example, one group drew a picture of a drunk causing a car accident); and finally they had to recite a piece of prose that they had learned. As I have mentioned previously, some of the older boys are tiring of these structured activities, and Chinzorig spent much of the time knocking a football around on the fringe of things.

In the afternoon, the German woman (Ulie) and I took a large group of children to collect berries. We were expecting one of the ger mothers to come with us, but we turned out to be on our own with nineteen kids, some of whom were quite small. To get to the trees we had to cross three rivers, the third of which was pretty deep (to my upper thighs) and fast flowing. I was very worried about the little ones, but we couldn't turn back, as some of the children had already crossed over ahead of us, and were now conveniently forgetting their English as I called for them to come back. So we waded perilously across – me with one child on my back, and holding the hand of another; Ulie with a child holding hands on either side of her. Even Galaa was carrying a little one on his back, although he wobbled precariously as he giggled his way over. We collected several bags of berries, and then had no choice but to return by the same route. I was particularly conscious of the disasters that have occurred in the west on children's trips, and I was very relieved when we got them all safely across and back to the Camp. Needless to say the kids all thought that it was great fun.

August 8

This is my last day in the Camp before Brenda arrives, and I can't wait to introduce her to everyone, and to show her where I have been working during the summer. But there are now two serious worries here – firstly the missing boy has still not turned up; and secondly Kinjay, the baby boy of the ex-Lotus girl who lives close to the Camp, has been taken to hospital with a very high temperature. As I have described previously, the standard of health care here leaves much to be desired, and everyone is very concerned about him. I have watched him develop over the weeks I have been here – at first he just slept most of the time, but now every time he sees me he gives me a lovely beaming smile. It would be awful if anything happened to him.

Elsewhere in the valley there has been a death, the third since I have been in the camp, and in accordance with tradition the children were given rice with raisins, plus sweets and drinks, by the bereaved family.

The children who went with Didi to the city are still away, so it is relatively quiet here at the moment. I did some reading with some of the children in the morning, and then played football with Chinzorig; his great friend Batra; little Basca, who looks and tackles like Denis Wise; Gantaluk the dancer, who plays in bare feet; and a few others. During a break from the footie one of the girls tried (with predictable results) to teach me one of the traditional dances!

In the early evening I went for a long contemplative walk in the mountains. I was on my way down, and passing a rocky hollow, when a wolf emerged from it only about twenty metres from me and started advancing with a low growl! Despite that fact that I have read many times that wolves do not attack humans, his teeth were a lot bigger than mine, and I was pretty frightened. I backed away, maintaining eye contact (I must have read that somewhere!). I also picked up a large stone, although I'm not quite sure exactly what I was planning to do with it! Fortunately he quickly got bored with scaring me, and just sat and looked at me while I beat a hasty retreat. I looked back as I got further down, and he was still sitting there staring in my direction. I breathlessly reported this to the Camp, but they showed little interest – apparently there are large numbers of wolves around, and a tethered horse was recently found killed by a pack.

After dinner I played chess with Chinzorig. I had brought the set into Camp just a few weeks previously, and all the instructions were in English. But already he has fully grasped the game, and was able to give me a good run for my money. No doubt this time next year he will be able to thrash me…

Later in the evening Osko and Zorig returned from their breaks, and as usual Osko had brought food with her which we ate in her ger after the kids had gone to bed. She also brought me presents – some photographs; a key ring; and a chess set with the board made from camel hair, and the pieces from sheeps' ankle bones. Throughout my time here I have been deeply touched by the kindness and generosity of the people I have met. It makes my own profession seem largely meaningless at present.

9 – SAYING GOODBYE

August 9

Got back to UB after lunch, and met an Israeli guy and a Russian guy in the Guest House, who are both travelling. As it was the last day in Mongolia for the two Dutch vets, Janika and Vipka, a group of us had already arranged to climb the hill that overlooks UB and watch the sunset, before going out to dinner. In the end there were nine of us: the two from the Guest House, the two vets, a Swiss guy in his mid-thirties who gave up his job in marketing six months ago, and who has been travelling ever since, Sian (who was with us in the Gobi), Del and Prisca, and me. We were a long time on the hill, which is about three kilometres out of town, and late coming back. Tongue in cheek, the Swiss guy flagged down an empty luxury coach. Amazingly, with a big grin, the driver stopped and gave us a lift back to the main square in UB, charging us less than 5p each!

Afterwards we had a lovely meal at a Korean restaurant, really splashing out, and spending just over 20 pounds for the nine of us! Western prices will come as a real shock in due course...

Janika and Vipka have both been staying with nomad families, and Janika's "host mother" has hand made for her a full length Mongolian coat (a "dell"), complete with braiding and decorations. It must have taken her very many hours of work. Her host father then blessed the dell with milk, in a formal ceremony in which it was presented to her. Janika was deeply moved – so many of the Mongolians we have met, especially outside the city, have been wonderfully welcoming and hospitable.

August 10

I went to Ananda for lunch and ran into two Englishmen who have just arrived, having driven from London in a 19 year old Ford

Fiesta. They followed much of the old Silk Road, driving through Uzbekhistan, Kazakhstan and Turkmenistan into Russia, before entering north western Mongolia across the Russian border. It took them 32 days. Mongolia was the most difficult section, as the roads are appalling, and I have no idea how they managed it in an old two wheel drive car, with limited ground clearance. They broke down two or three times, but miraculously, the nomads who came across them were always able to help, and fix the problem. At one point they broke a spring about three days away from UB, and within four hours a Mongolian who spoke not a word of English had managed to find and fit a replacement! They showed me a video clip of a young herdsman directing them through a river crossing – at one point the water lapped the bonnet, but they just made it across. The alternative would have taken them several days out of their way.

They have been sponsored for the journey and have raised more than 5,000 pounds for Lotus. It's a remarkable achievement, entirely on their own and without back-up. Check out their website at www.overlandfiesta.co.uk. They have posted photographs and video clips on it. They are driving back "the short way" via Moscow, which they reckon will take nine days. Piece of cake...

August 11

Today I checked out of the Guest House for the last time, as I am moving to a hotel for Brenda's arrival. The Guest House owner and her son insisted on giving me lunch before they would let me go – they have been very kind to me on each of my return visits to the city.

So Brenda arrives first thing Sunday morning, and then we go together to the Camp on Monday afternoon. It will be so good to be able to share some of my experiences with her.

August 12

Picked up Brenda from the airport, the dreaded Tupolov from Moscow having arrived bang on time. Checked into the luxurious Ulaanbaatar Hotel!

After breakfast we took the bus to the orphanage, where Umesh and, in particular, Ankhar, were delighted to see us. I feel sorry for Ankhar, who is basically fine, although he does need attention. But he has been left kicking his heels with the little ones for the last month, having been sent back from the Camp, and clearly has little to do there. He mentioned to me the mountains, and swimming, and I can't help thinking he would be much better off in the country. Didi has told me there is some prospect of finding him adoptive parents amongst the nomad community, and this would suit him perfectly.

Also there was the older special needs girl (who you will remember once threatened to kill me) and who was fascinated by my longer hair, and the fact that I no longer have a beard. I also saw Ariumbata, who they have finally decided is too difficult to keep in the Camp, and who in any event was getting nothing out of it. But the really good news was that the missing boy (whose name is impossible to write) has also finally turned up there. This is a great relief. We stayed for a couple of hours, were given lunch (vegetables and strips of dough – the latter to provide "bulk" for the kids), and then went to the local shop with Ankhar and another boy to buy them ice-creams.

In the evening we dropped into a restaurant to say good-bye to Sian, who was having dinner with some of the Mongolian vets with whom she has been working. She leaves for London first thing in the morning.

August 13

Got to the Camp at four in the afternoon to the usual wonderful welcome. Everyone was particularly pleased to meet Brenda, who fitted in immediately – playing and laughing with the children. Enkhee has adapted the teaching ger for us – with two mattresses (moderately clean) side by side on the floor, a cupboard for our rucksacks, a stove, and pictures by the children on the walls. True luxury – but I have to say I rather miss the dirty, cold, infested ger where I have spent the summer. Amazing how we can adapt to such basic living.

There are eight new children here, ranging from two to fourteen, part of a group of about 40 street kids who have been held by the police for many weeks, because there is nowhere else to put them. They have effectively been imprisoned – not going out at all, and having tiny grilles for windows in their accommodation. Didi would like to take them all, but right now simply does not have the space available, so will take this group for a week, and then another group the next week, and so on. By the end of their first day, two of the older ones had already absconded, and were found making their way back to UB. Didi is very philosophical about that – if that is what they want, then she must accept it. Mongolian children are, on the whole, much more independent than their British counterparts, and are capable of making decisions about their lives much earlier than they would in the west.

I was expecting the new kids to be wild – but they have fitted in relatively well, and have been split up around the gers in accordance with their ages. So although inevitably they are a bit reticent, already they are beginning to fit in into camp life. What does make them stand out is that many of them have nasty skin problems, and several have shaven heads to allow scabs and sores to heal. A week at the Camp will do them a tremendous amount of good, and long term Didi is hopeful of finding room for all of them.

In the early evening, the children put on their costumes, and staged a wonderful concert of song and dance especially for Brenda and me. I felt very emotional. They danced and sang beautifully – especially Gantaluk, who was at his astonishing best. Didi is hoping to send him early next year to a specialist school for dance and drama, where his exceptional talent will have full opportunity to express itself. He has been transformed from the difficult, unco-operative street kid of a year ago, to a 13 year old with a future full of possibilities, and who is kind and generous to the younger children. He is also a highly talented footballer, who invariably plays in bare feet, and is so quick he can leave 2 or 3 of the others standing in the space of 10 metres! After the concert, and as it grew dark, we had a disco, Zorig having borrowed a generator from an adjoining ger. The children loved it, and towards the end some of them started to do acrobatics and gymnastics on a long felt mat. Brenda was astonished at their strength and agility – there was a little boy of about eight (Jackie) who effortlessly went into the yoga "scorpion" posture. In thirty years of practising and teaching yoga she has never seen anyone do this before – she has only seen photographs of it in books. From where do the kids get such talent?

We had taken sausage and bread, plus a bottle of wine, plus fresh mango, back to the Camp with us this time, and after the children had gone to bed we retired to Osko's ger, and consumed this with Enkhee, Osko, Zorig, Ulie, Nyamaa, Oyuna, and some Singaporeans who have come to the Camp to organise activities with the children for the next week. Zorig grinned hugely when I produced the wine, remembering our trials in opening the previous bottle we had drunk. He mimed my efforts to force the cork down with a spike! Enkhee and Osko said some lovely things about my contribution during the summer, and I was especially touched by their comment that there was always a happy atmosphere about the Camp when I was there. Enkhee spoke of my kindness, and the love the children have for me. Not for the first time in Mongolia I felt very humble. I do hope I have been able to add something to their lives while briefly passing through.

August 14

My last full day in the Camp. Chinzorig has been playing football all through the summer in boots at least three sizes too big for him, so I had bought him new gold and black (fake) Adidas boots in the black market in UB. I also gave to Batra my Arsenal shirt (with "Henry" on the back), which I had always worn when playing. They were both really delighted and wore them to play that morning.

Brenda and I went for a long walk in the mountains, and then in the afternoon I played cards with some of the children in the activity tent (the "blue tent"), and Brenda helped some others make "friendship" bracelets. After a while more and more kids came into the blue tent, and Basca (he of the Denis Wise looks and tackle) asked me to do a rap! As much to my astonishment as theirs I improvised the "Basca Rap", and then progressed to scat singing! The children (now about thirty of them) all joined in and clapped faster and faster as I completely let myself go – you lose all your inhibitions in a place like this. It was really good fun, and the kids loved it!!

That night we were again invited into Osko's ger, and Zorig, Enkhee, and one of the ger mothers who has a particularly beautiful voice, all sang traditional and modern Mongolian songs for us as we passed round the vodka. We went to bed in our ger for the last time at midnight. It was a magical evening. I will miss them hugely.

August 15

Although I didn't sleep well last night, we were determined to make the last few hours in the Camp fun. I had asked Enkhee to try to make sure that all of the ger mothers and the children were at the morning circle, and after the usual exercises I just said a few words of thanks to everyone, and promised that I would be coming back (which I most certainly will). Brenda then led a rousing version of the Hokey Cokey (which the kids loved!), and I finished with two choruses of "*Everywhere we go....people always ask us......*" I had done it just once previously with them, but about 80 children all joined in and at the end belted out "MIGHTY MIGHTY MIGHTY MIGHTY MIGHTY MIGHTY LOTUS!!!". Wonderful stuff.

We then had to wait several hours for the car, and the children mostly hung around us, making more friendship bracelets and presenting them to us, and drawing pictures for us. Gantaluk disappeared for about 15 minutes and then reappeared with a quite wonderful coloured drawing of three dancers which he had done on a piece of cardboard that he had found somewhere. It is superb. I can't wait to see what he is doing when I come back.

Chinzorig hardly left my side all the time – we had spoken quietly the previous day, when he said that he would miss me. I told him that it was fine to cry, and that I would do so, but I know it is not really within the male Mongolian culture to display feelings in that way.

When the car finally came to take us back to UB it was one of the most emotional experiences of my life. It was very, very hard. Poor Galaa clearly couldn't deal with it, and although he is always in evidence around the Camp, he had taken himself off somewhere so that his tears couldn't be seen. I had to respect his decision, and I left him, and said to goodbye to the others in turn. Enkhee, Osko and Nyamaa have promised to come to the station to see us off on Friday. I kept the tears at bay until I was inside the car. As we drove away they all stood and waved, but I noticed Chinzorig run from the group and go to his ger.

In the evening back in UB we met Gek and her partner David for dinner, and were joined afterwards by Didi. We chatted until midnight. Didi is one of the most remarkable and caring human beings I have ever met. Her designated role within the Ananda order is to care for the street children and this has become her life's work. What is achieved at Lotus is quite astonishing. She takes in children from the most desperate backgrounds, and by her own example creates a loving and caring home for them which gives them the opportunity to lead lives away from the street, and to discover their skills and their self esteem. Their education is vital, and the primary school that she runs alongside the orphanage has a wonderful and vibrant atmosphere to it that turns out happy, bright, and largely well adjusted children, despite all of their problems. Looking ahead I will do my very best to help her in probably the best way I can, which is with fund raising, as the lack of money is always a problem for her. Clearly she has endured some heartbreaking experiences. She described to me the suicide of one of her children, and although this was now sometime ago, it was obvious that it still hurts her, and she feels guilt that it happened. But I guess her long training has taught her a detachment which enables her to get through the tragedies. She of all people cannot fall apart whatever may happen, for the sake of all the other children in her care.

And so in a few hours we will take the train to Siberia, and after a few days by Lake Baikal it is the Trans-Siberian Express for three days and nights until finally we arrive in Moscow. My thoughts on Mongolia are many and varied. On the one hand, especially in the city, there is corruption, unemployment, alcoholism and domestic violence. On the other hand there is the stunning beauty and remoteness of the countryside; the genuine warmth and generosity of the nomadic community, seeking nothing in return; and the outstanding potential and talent of the people and country as a whole.

What have I been able to give to the children? A little English; kindness; affection; and my time. What have Mongolians, and especially those in the Camp given to me? Their hospitality; their generosity; their wonderful smiles; their happiness in having me around them; their love. They have reminded me of the priorities of life. I have remembered what is important, and how fortunate

I am compared to so many. The children have taught me how to overcome terrible disadvantage and still be positive, and to use their many talents to the full. I have learnt humility. It has been an honour and a privilege to live amongst them. I will never forget them. Of all the wonderful people I have met my particular thanks go to Didi, who devotes the whole of her life to the children; Del, who has become such a good friend; Enkhee; Osko; Zorig; Nyamaa; Galaa; Chinzorig; Batra, Chinza's great friend; Ariunzea; Gantaluk the dancer; Uurganaa; Umesh; tough little Basca, who told me yesterday how much he loved me; Inkhzaya, with the lovely smile; and her little sister Inkhchumick. They are truly amazing.

August 17

We got up early on our last morning to climb Zaisan Hill outside the city, to get a last view over UB. I found it a very difficult night, knowing what I was leaving behind. We did a bit of shopping in the morning, and then went to the station. There waiting for us were Enkhee, Osko, Nyamaa and one of the other ger mothers. Enkhee told me that Galaa had stayed very much on his own the day we left the Camp, but had been a bit better that morning. Nyamaa had been to the orphanage and said that Ankhar sent his love, and had wished us a safe journey. I had written a letter to Chinzorig, which I gave to Enkhee.

They then gave to us two bags filled with bread, cheese, sausage, gherkins, warm buuz (Mongolian dumplings stuffed with mutton), beer, water, chocolate, dried yoghourt, and airag – the fermented mare's milk beloved of the nomads. In short, they had made sure we had everything we needed for the journey. Once again their kindness overwhelmed me, and there were more tears as we waved good-bye.

The train to the Russian border took about seven hours, and we passed through the most remarkable countryside I have ever seen. Thousands of square kilometres of pure unspoilt steppe.

The only signs of human habitation were a few gers dotted about and, at one point, a nomad herding camels on horseback.

It took us six hours to cross the border as Russian beaurocracy took over from Mongolian hospitality. Then it was a further eleven hours to Irkutsk, from where we took a taxi to Lake Baikal. This is the largest freshwater lake in the world by capacity. If all of the world's drinking water ran out tomorrow, then there would be sufficient water in Lake Baikal to supply drinking water to the population of the entire world for 40 years (if it could be moved!).

It is lovely here, but it is not Mongolia ...

SUMMER 2008

MONGOLIA REVISITED

June 21

"*You'll never get those kids out of your head*". So wrote my good friend Brian in a comment on my blog on 6 June 2007. At the time I'd only been in Mongolia for six days. How could he have known? I've no idea, but he was certainly right.

In September last year I returned to my "day job" as a corporate lawyer, but, although I am well aware that it's a cliché, I had had a life changing experience. The first thing I set about doing was to form as a UK charity "The Lotus Children's Centre Charitable Trust". Didi had asked me to do this in order to help promote Lotus in England, and also so that it could be used as a fund-raising vehicle. I was honoured to be asked to be one of the Trustees, along with Didi, Bratatii (her Australian friend I wrote about previously), Cathy Lee, another sister from the Ananda order who works at a school in Laos, and Maria Wells, an English teacher, who had run the Lotus primary school for two years, and who is now back in England. Due to the usual bureaucracy, and the need to collect signatures from around the world, it took about six months to get the charity registered, but that was finally achieved in February this year.

In the meantime, Didi had made her first visit ever to England, and it was lovely to see her a couple of times. On one evening we met Annie Smith, a trustee of the Onaway Trust, who promised to give us all the help she could. A few weeks ago I made an application to the Onaway Trust for funding assistance with the setting up of a Summer Camp for the Lotus children in Erdenet, a town in the north of Mongolia. We have been lucky enough to receive a grant from them of £4,500, towards the overall cost of £8,000, which means that these children (there are currently 17 of them) can enjoy the same sort of summer facilities as the Lotus children in Ulaanbaatar. Work will start straight away, and I am hoping to get the chance to go there in the next two weeks.

I was also able to get the new Trust registered with Charity Challenge, the agency specialising in organising fund raising treks and bike rides for various charities. I am trekking in the Indian Himalayas in November, and people have been incredibly generous in their sponsorship. Generally speaking the response we have received everywhere to the story of the Lotus children has been fantastic – a school in Sevenoaks raised £750, Brian and Julie in France had a book sale which raised £350, and we have had several donations from Rotary Clubs; where I give a brief talk, and show slides of the country and the children.

As you will have deduced from the above, Brenda and I catch a flight back to Ulaanbaatar this evening to spend two weeks with the children, and it will be a very emotional experience. Will Galaa remember me? How's Ariunzea getting on at school? Has Gantaluk been able to get into the College of Dance, or has he lost interest a year down the line? I hope not, because he has great talent. I have missed them, and Enkhmaa, who works as a book-keeper at Lotus, and with whom I have exchanged emails, tells me that they have missed me.

I was able to email the Chinggis Guest House, where I stayed when I was in the city last year, and the owner (Saikhnaa) was delighted to hear from me, and so we are booked in there for the first three nights. She and her family were really kind to me when I stayed there last year, and it will be good to see them again.

We then plan to go the Sumer Camp, where Brenda will teach yoga, and I will resume my attempts to masquerade as an English teacher – fortified by the TEFL course that I did earlier this year. However, I gather there has been "hand, foot and mouth" disease in Terelj, so the children haven't yet gone down. Apparently this is a highly contagious disease that spreads from the cattle population to humans, and large gatherings of people in Terelj are currently banned. We are all hoping that they will finally get there next week, as it gives them the freedom that they lack in the cramped conditions of the Centre.

Now I need to complete my packing – we are taking tons of games, clothes and shoes for the kids, so although Korean Air have given us an additional allowance of 20 kilos, there is not much space for our stuff! I hope to continue the blog when we get there. I'm really excited!

June 22

Having experienced the dreaded Tupolov last year, and having been told by Didi that three of them went down in Eastern Europe the previous winter, we decided this year to use Korean Air, and go via Seoul. As soon as we saw the cabin staff we knew we were right – smiling, friendly, helpful girls; as opposed to the fierce looking ex-shot putters on Aeroflot. And all remained well as we approached UB, with me experiencing a tingling excitement, as well as a certain apprehension (I've no idea why). Ten minutes from landing, we were told that there was some unexpected bad weather, and we would be circling for a few minutes. Ninety minutes later we were told that we would be diverting to Beijing. When we got there, instead of disembarking, we were told we would wait for the weather to clear in UB, and then fly back...

....five hours later, we were told we would be returning to Seoul! So here I am, well over 30 hours after we left home, and with another 11 hours to wait before we have another go. Sigh! Frustrating to say the least, and we are very tired. Apparently our bags have been unloaded, and will be moved to the new plane later on today. Let's hope there is no problem there, as we would not want to lose all the clothes, games, toys etc. that we have brought for the children.

The worst bit is that Bratatii flies out later today, and I think we will certainly miss her. That is a real shame, as I was looking forward to seeing her again, and we were planning to have a trustees' meeting today. Maybe we can do it by skype, but it's not the same as chatting things over face to face.

I hope to be able to report more positively tomorrow. Right now I'm going to try to get some sleep. Brenda is already well away...

June 23

Having spent another twelve hours in Seoul, we finally took off again at 8pm on Monday evening. We had the same seats as on the Seoul/UB/Beijing/Seoul flight the previous day, which were right at the back. The disadvantage of those seats is that they serve you last. So for the third consecutive meal we were first offered the choice of three delicious sounding main dishes, only to be told "*We are very sorry – all we have left is Korean Rice*" So very Pythonesque – "*Spam and eggs, Spam and chips, or Spam on its own!*"

Finally landed at UB at about 11pm, and were met by Otgoo from Projects Abroad, who had organised things for me last year. But not before we had our bags searched by a very severe, obviously Russian trained, female Mongolian customs officer, who clearly found it hard to believe that we were carrying three large bags filled mainly with second hand clothes and games for the kids. She was most suspicious, and it was only after a detailed inquisition that she finally relented and let us through.

There was another mini-drama on the way to the Guest House, when we were stopped by the Police, and unfortunately the driver did not have the correct papers with him, as the car had been borrowed from Oko, the local director of Projects Abroad. The driver was asked to leave the car, and the policeman climbed in, apparently intending to impound it and all its contents! There followed a lengthy negotiation between Otgoo and the policeman, which ended in a wad of money being passed from the former to the latter, and we all went on our way (tolerably) happy.

Saikhnaa, the owner of the Guest House, has put us an apartment about five minutes walk from the Post Office, which we share with four others, and which is very comfortable. We went to bed tired, but glad to have arrived.

June 24

We woke up to pouring rain, and heard that it had been raining for the last four days, and showed no sign of relenting. I phoned Didi, and discovered the good news that Bratatii was not due to leave until the following day. We agreed to meet with her, Bratatii, and Cathy Lee (who I had not met before), at the Lotus vegetarian café for a formal meeting of the trustees of the UK Trust, which we have to hold a least once a year. Afterwards we chatted generally about the children. They are all fine, and apparently very excited about my coming back. Chinzorig had asked to come to the airport to meet me, but he was stuck out at the summer camp, which has turned out to be a bit of a nightmare so far. After the valley was declared safe from the "hand foot and mouth" disease the kids finally went out there the previous Friday, but it started raining hard. By Monday morning the Tuul River had broken its banks, and was lapping at the front gers. By Monday afternoon almost all of the kids had been evacuated leaving a skeleton occupancy of Chinzorig, Batra, one other boy, and Enkhee. The rain is good news for the herdsmen in the valley, who had been suffering from a draught, but bad news for the children, who love the space and freedom that the Camp gives them.

Didi asked us to go back to the café at 8.00 in the evening as there is a serious dispute with the adjoining owner. On the previous night he had built a wall in front of his own premises but encroaching at least three feet onto the steps of the Ananda café, and boxing it into a very narrow space. He had also broken the poles (like those that prop up a ger) which form a feature at the front of the café. The guy turned up shortly after 8 and immediately started shouting at one of Didi's staff, who was there as a translator. We told him the wall had to be moved back on to his land and that he should repair the poles. Unfortunately his response was both threatening and abusive. After about half an hour we were clearly getting nowhere and went back into the café. He followed us in and continued to shout abuse until finally we were able to calm him down a bit and usher him out of the door. Didi is very cross, but probably has no remedy as if she sought help from the Courts the likelihood is that the determination would depend on who offered the largest bribe!

I also met during the day, Ben, a volunteer from an Australian aid organisation who is working at Lotus for a year trying to (re) organise the administrative side of things. We were discussing how tough the kids are, and he told me that he had been playing basketball outside his apartment last week and a boy fell and shattered his arm. There were no tears at all as he was taken off to hospital, and the other lads just shrugged their shoulders and got on with the game!

Didi had with her in the evening a tiny baby, who has been borne with a hole in the heart. Whether or not that is the reason we don't know, but her mother promptly abandoned her, and at one week old she found her way to Lotus. She is now eleven weeks, and doing fine. She was premature, and it seems that the hole may have healed naturally. But there is no sign of her mother. She apparently comes from a region where the first name of the people is traditionally "Dalai", which means "Ocean" (Dalai Lama – "Ocean of Knowledge"). The baby has been called "Ocean of Happiness".

After dinner we strolled back to our apartment and despite the wall incident I still felt a tremendous sense of wellbeing at being back in Mongolia, and excitement that tomorrow we will go to the Centre and see the children again.

June 25

"*I do shits now...*" "*I'm sorry?*" "*I do shits now...*" said Saikhnaa to me at 1am this morning as I wandered back to our room in my boxers having visited the toilet in the middle of the night. With that she scooped up the bed linen and was gone. Saikhnaa works incredibly hard – she runs the main Guest House, with two dormitories and two double rooms; plus two other apartments, each with three rooms. People tend to stay in UB for very short periods – off the Trans Sib for a two or three day break, and then back on it again. So she is for ever changing the sheets, and cleaning the three premises. On top of that she does her visitors' washing as well (for one dollar a load), so she seems to get very little sleep. But she has reaped the rewards of her hard work in the new capitalist Mongolia, and the three apartments are now probably worth at least US$200k.

After breakfast, Brenda and I took the bus out into the Yarmag shanty town to the Lotus Centre. I had a rather odd knot in my stomach as I approached. As I entered the yard I saw children playing on the trampoline and others just running and jumping and letting off steam. Uurganaa saw me first, and with a sudden shout of "*FRASER*" he jumped into my arms. After that it was a whirlwind of hugs and kisses and high fives as the children raced over to say hello. Welcomed as if I'd never been gone. As if they'd always known I'd come back, and here I was. Just undemanding, uncomplicated, love. No wonder this place has changed me.

The ger mothers from the summer camp also all came over and greeted me with smiles and laughter. The bad news is that my music teacher friend from last time, Zorig, has reverted to drinking heavily, and although Didi has kept him on, it is becoming a serious problem, as he can become quite aggressive. I doubt that I will see him during this visit.

Ankhar and Umesh soon became my shadows as I wandered around the place taking it all in again. Ariunzea came to talk to us, and her English, always good, is now better than ever. She is very fond of Brenda, and soon took her off to show her where she slept (on the floor, in a crowded room, but which is kept immaculately by the older girls and their ger mother).

As we chatted to Didi a little girl of five or six came over, and Didi told us that she had been aborted at about 24 weeks, and borne just under two pounds. She has half of one ear missing where it was burnt in the incubator, and the mother then abandoned her. She came to Lotus at six weeks old, and is now a happy thriving little girl.

Outside I saw the baby borne blind with syphilis who I mentioned last year – now with her sight completely restored and toddling around in the yard; tumbling over and then struggling up again. Because she was relatively immobile for some time she is behind in her walking, but otherwise seems fine.

I didn't see Galaa who was at the other house where some of the older boys live, but I'll see him next time. The weather forecast is not good, and Didi doesn't know when she will be able to get the children back to the Camp. So for the time being Brenda and I will stay in UB and go up to the Centre and play with and chat to the children.

In the evening we had dinner with Monbhat, a local consultant who is a good friend of David Allen, the chairman of DHL, and who I had met in London. David has been instrumental in setting up a kidney dialysis unit in UB, and in funding and organising the training in Korea of a Mongolian transplant surgeon, who has now successfully carried out twenty kidney transplants. The next step is liver transplants, and the training will again be funded by David and his friends. They are keen to help Lotus, and so a very good contact. The hotel group, Six Senses, have asked me if there would be an appropriate site in the countryside for a luxury resort. Six Senses' policy is to build their resorts using local materials and labour, and staff it with local people. They always give back at least 2% of gross revenue to local communities. They are building (in Turkey) the first totally carbon neutral resort in the world, and are just the sort of developer that Mongolia needs. They would bring some wealth and skills to the local community, but without damaging the pristine environment of the steppe.

I discussed this with Monhbat, and he believes that there is an appropriate site available about 200 kilometres from the City, that has the advantage of hot springs that could be used for the spa, and for heating in the winter. He will try to take me to see it before I go.

Tomorrow we have meetings regarding the new Lotus Centre which Didi is hoping to build, as the existing premises are cramped and unhealthy, and have a limited life span. Some good progress has been made in fundraising, but there are issues regarding the title to the site, and other matters that we will attempt to deal with in the next day or so.

The weather forecast is not good, so we are unlikely to get to the summer camp for a few days yet.

June 26

Ego, ambition, desire for power. All precisely the opposite of the way Didi lives her life, but sadly they have rudely intruded into it. We had two meetings yesterday in connection with the proposal to build a new Lotus Centre, and all that I can say on an open blog is that they were highly instructive. Further meetings are planned for next week.

The meetings took up much of the day, but we did have time to adjourn with Didi (and Ocean of Happiness) to the Ananda Café for lunch. There, Didi told us in greater detail than before the story of one of the children who came to her very young. She had been at Lotus for about ten months when her mother came to take her back. Nothing more was heard until Didi received a visit about seven months later from the little girl's grandfather. Apparently her mother had exchanged her for a new ger, but her new "adoptive parents" were unable to cope with her. She cried all the time, refused to eat, and just clung on to a set of beads, which they were unable to prise away from her without causing a crescendo of screaming. Her grandfather was sure she was dying, and Didi went to see her. As soon as she heard Didi's voice the little girl turned to her and stopped crying. After a long negotiation Didi was allowed to take the child back to Lotus, where she is now five years old, and doing fine. The beads had been put on her by Didi when she was tiny.

We have walked right into the last few days of campaigning for the Mongolian general election, which takes place this Sunday. There are over 350 candidates for 63 seats, and there are cars with flags and loudspeakers parading up and down the streets of UB all the time. Although there are a large number of fringe parties involved, the fight is really between the Communists and the Democrats. But the distinction between the two is much narrower than you might think – both believe in the free market economy, and there is now no turning back from capitalism for Mongolia.

In the evening we saw Osko, the dance teacher from last year's Camp. She retired at the end of last term, and I wasn't sure that we would be seeing her. However, I'm glad to say that she got my mobile number from somewhere, and called to say "*I want see you now!*" She brought with her gifts of Mongolian liqueur, biscuits, and fruit juice, and (if we have the time) we will be visiting her apartment next week, when she has promised to cook us a Mongolian dinner.

June 27

We spent a restless night listening to a lot of questionable nocturnal activity outside our window, and did not really sleep properly until after dawn. We dragged ourselves out of bed at about 9:30, and after breakfast went back up to the Centre. I went over to the "Boys House", which is about 10 minutes walk from the main Centre, to see Galaa. To my surprise he remembered me – as I walked into the yard his face lit up, and he came racing over. "*Hello Fraser, how are you?*" he said, as indeed he had said every day in the Camp for three months last summer! "*I'm fine, Galaa, how are you?*" "*Mehtque*" (I don't know) was his stock reply, as he had now exhausted his supply of English! It was good to see him again – he will never grow up (he is about 20 now), but he has a lovely sunny nature, although he is rather isolated from the other older boys.

Back in the main Centre Brenda went off to help in an art class, and I kicked a ball around with Basca and one of the other lads. Suddenly there was a bit of a commotion, and a crash, and I saw Gantaluk struggling to support Umesh. He was having a severe epileptic fit, and the smaller children were very frightened. We managed to get him to lie down and then he passed out completely. We put him in the shade, and one of the ger mothers sponged his forehead with a wet towel. His pulse was very fast to start with, and he was hot. But gradually his body settled down, and he slept for about four hours, after which he seemed much better. He carries tablets all the time for his epilepsy, and can usually feel a fit coming on and take a tablet before he passes out. This time it appears to have taken him by surprise.

The Lotus children are taking part this year in the opening parade of the Naadam Festival on July 11. The opening ceremony fills the National Stadium to its 10,000 capacity, and the kids are very excited. We accompanied them back into the City this evening for a rehearsal. They had all been well scrubbed and had on their best clothes. They looked great, and I was very proud of them!

Tomorrow we go out to the Summer Camp for one night to see Chinzorig, Batra and Enkhee. The weather has still not properly relented, and there is no sign of the other children going back there yet.

On Sunday we go to Erdenet with Didi to see the Lotus Centre there, and to agree the final arrangements for the Summer Camp that is being put in place outside the city.

June 28

Today the plan was to take a bus out to Terelj, walk to the Summer Camp, and then stay overnight with the three children who had stayed behind. However, we got a call early on from Didi to tell us that they had all come back this morning, except for one ger mother who was left looking after the place. So instead we took a taxi to the Black Market (Naraantuul) to see if we could get some colouring books for the kids, and also to check on the price of winter boots, as someone had said that they were in very short supply at Lotus.

The weather at last was beautiful this morning – sunny and maybe 30 degrees – and more like what I expected from a Mongolian summer. We set off in shorts and tee shirts, delighted to feel the warmth on our backs. We tracked down the colouring books, and bought 30 of them. We also discovered that 50 pairs of warm winter boots could be bought for about 250 pounds. The idea is for Brenda to hold a yoga day back home to raise the money for them

We lunched in the market at a Mongolian "greasy spoon", trusting our bowels to stand firm, and ate buuz (mutton dumplings) and potato salad. It was delicious!

The sky had been darkening steadily, and as we left the market the heavens opened, with lightning dramatically darting across the sky. We managed to pick up a taxi that took us back into town, and then hopped straight on a bus up to the Lotus Centre. It was pouring when we got there, and the road that led to Lotus had been turned into a raging torrent of water. It was completely impassable – I have never seen anything like it. People were desperately trying to keep the water out of their homes, but in some cases to no avail as it poured through their gers and houses, and flushed the pit toilets.

Having got that far we didn't want to turn back, so we tracked back to the tarmac road, and then took a long detour to approach the township from the other side. I wasn't at all sure how sensible we were being as we slipped and slithered in the mud, long since soaked to the skin. But my sense of direction stood the test, and finally we found Lotus, having approached it from the opposite direction. It was worth it. As we ducked inside one of the boys called to Chinzorig, who we had not seen since we arrived, as he had been at the Camp. He ran over and we hugged each other. It was great to see him again. The three of us then sat in the office and chatted to him while Brenda and I tried to dry off.

Didi has told me that Chinza is not going to school, and I talked about it to him. He says that he has no friends there, and that when he stopped going because he was ill the teacher did not believe him, and that "*she doesn't like me*". He said that he might prefer to go to the government school (because he is exceptionally bright he is one of only two children at Lotus who goes to a private school), and that maybe he would start going again if he could move. We asked him what he would like to do in later life, and he said he would like to become an architect. He understands that to do that he has to pass the exams, but clearly he has significant problems at the moment and life is not easy for him. I do hope he gets back on track somehow, as he is a kind and caring person, who has the talent to achieve whatever he wants. He had made a small bag for us on which he had embroidered our names. Apparently he stayed up all night to finish it. This place is capable of touching the emotions like no other.

In a pause in the rain we made our way back to UB, promising to see them all again on Tuesday. All being well we are expecting to go to Erdenet tomorrow with Didi, but this is Mongolia, so who knows?

June 29

After some delay in the morning while Didi tried to arrange a meeting, we set off for Erdenet at about 12:45, and were delighted to find that Chinzorig and Batra were coming with us, as well as Tsutappa, who is effectively Didi's "second in command". About five kilometres outside the City we stopped to see "The Potato Farm", which turns out to be a smallholding owned by Lotus, where the children learn to grow potatoes which they then take back to the Centre – potatoes are a major part of their diet. There is a small wooden house on the site (very run down!) where an old lady used to live, but she is now in an old people's hospital. Having seen something of the hospitals on my last visit, I dread to think what conditions are like in the geriatric homes.

Because the kids had been prevented by the "hand, foot and mouth" disease from going to the summer camp at the beginning of June, and because the heavy rain had driven them back when they finally got there a couple of weeks ago, Didi had sent some of the older boys to The Potato Farm for ten days. At least while they were there they were able to taste some clean air, and there is enough space for them to play football alongside the smallholding. They erected a temporary ger on the site, as the wooden shack is not big enough to house the boys, and a ger mother stayed there to look after them.

We then drove north across the vast undulating steppe, before crossing a river just south of Darkhan, and heading west towards Erdenet. After another hour we stopped at a ramshackle town called Khoutoo, where Didi is setting up a "youth café". There is nothing at all for kids to do in this incredibly drab, Russian built, town, and so there is a very high level of teenage alcoholism. Didi bought an apartment there last year for U.S.$7,000 (now worth twice as much), has renovated it in bright lively colours, installed a kitchen and bathroom, and built a wooden patio. All the plasterwork and painting was done by the older Lotus girls in

UB, and it looks terrific. The café is now just about ready to open, and will be staffed initially by one western volunteer, who will live in a tiny room on site, and by local girls. Apart from providing an essential facility for the local young people, it will also provide work for two or three others. Didi's resourcefulness and imagination never ceases to amaze me!

We finally arrived in Erdenet at about 7:30. It is the second largest town in Mongolia, and dominated by the slag heap from the copper mine. The town was built by the Russians in 1974 and is not pretty, but less run down than I had been expecting. The mine is the lifeblood of the town, and employs nearly 8,000 people.

There are 17 children aged between five and 15 living in two Lotus apartments, looked after by one house mother. They greeted us with the usual Mongolian smiles and chatter, but don't seem to speak much English. Didi pointed out one little boy of about five whose mother wanted to take him back, until Didi discovered that she wanted to sell him. How desperate must the poor woman have been? Most of the children in the Erdenet Lotus are from backgrounds of alcoholism and/or prostitution.

After supper of vegetable soup, Didi, Brenda and I took three of the children to a park near to the apartment. The space is nice, and we played with a frisbee, and ran and chased the kids. But the carousel has to be pushed by hand (with great effort), and the other play equipment is either broken, or has been stolen. It has an atmosphere of decay. One of the children who came with us is Ogoo, who is seven and exceptionally bright and confident. He told us stories all the time illustrated by vivid mime. Apparently he has won the Erdenet poetry competition for his age group every year since he was able to take part, and he should go far.

Back in the apartments the children went to bed at about 11:00, and we joined them – sleeping on wooden bunks with no mattress, and only our sleeping bags to provide any comfort. Surprisingly we slept well.

June 30

Before leaving the town, Didi took Brenda and me to visit the site of the proposed summer camp for the Erdenet children, and for which (as I described earlier) I was able to raise funding from the UK based Onaway Trust. It is about 20 kilometres from the town centre, set in woodland on the side of a hill in a lovely alpine-like location, surrounded by meadows full of wild flowers. Really quite unlike anything else I had seen in Mongolia – much softer. I climbed the hill at the back of the site, and the hills and mountains beyond seemed to stretch forever, with no sign of human habitation, apart from the occasional white ger dotting the valleys. I took lots of photographs to send back to the people at Onaway.

On the way back to UB Didi told us about the tiny baby (about one month old) who Brenda and I had met a couple of days earlier at the Centre in UB. Apparently she was borne in May to one of the Lotus girls who is just 16, and who conceived her following a relationship with one of the boys at the Camp last summer. I remember there being some concern about the couple when I was here, and the boy was moved back into the city – obviously too late! They had both walked out of Lotus during the winter, and the father had got some sort of job. But after the baby was borne they found it too difficult, and have just turned up again complete with baby girl. Didi is trying to find a ger for them to live in, but it will be very difficult for them to hold the relationship together, and the prospects for them at the moment are not good.

We arrived back in UB in the evening, and tomorrow I have a meeting in connection with the prospective Six Senses resort.

July 1

I was supposed to have a meeting this morning with the owner of a site about 200 kilometres from UB, which enjoys the benefit of natural hot springs, and which may be a suitable site for an eco-friendly Six Senses resort. The meeting was in fact delayed in true Mongolian style until about noon, but the presentation I was given was very impressive and highly professional. I will take the information, plus a CD describing the project, back to Six Senses, and see what they think. I have no doubt that the company would be very supportive towards Lotus if they did build a resort in the area, and I am cautiously optimistic.

Afterwards we had lunch in a Dutch café, and heard about the election results. The first reports indicate that the MPRP (Communist Party) have won 44 out of 76 seats, with the Democrats claiming 21. The turnout is estimated at over 80%, which is astonishing in a country where much of the population live so far from the seat of government. We in the UK should be ashamed of our turnouts of about 50%. Maybe it stems from all those years of Russian domination when there was no freedom to vote at all? Having at last been given the opportunity to exercise their democratic rights, the people are not going to waste those rights.

The bedrock of MPRP support is in the countryside, where they have campaigned hard. There has also been some bribery involved – the government has been negotiating mining contracts with foreign companies such as Rio Tinto. This will generate significant income for the country, and the Democrats promised each adult Mongolian that they would receive a cash payment of $1,000 from the proceeds of the mining contracts. The MPRP promptly trumped that by offering $1,500 each, and, surprise surprise, guess who the people voted for? That sort of money can be the equivalent of 9/12 months' income for a Mongolian family.

In practice, the election result will change little. Prior to this there was a coalition between the MPRP and the Democrats, but the former held most of the positions of real power.

After lunch I phoned Tsutappa, who told me that the children are going back to the Summer Camp this evening. We have a meeting first thing with Didi, and then we will join them. I am sad it will only be for two nights, as we fly home just after midnight on Friday, but it will still be lovely to be back there. Enkhee is again the Camp Manager, and it will be very special to see her again. I am looking forward to it.

July 1 – evening

I never thought I'd see anything like it in peace-loving, welcoming Mongolia. Riot shields, tear gas, and rubber bullets. As I described in my earlier entry, the Communist Party appears to have won the election easily, but amongst the urban poor there is disbelief and anger. This was the first election in Mongolia to be held on the PR system, so that on each ballot paper voters could select three candidates in order of priority. Many people have failed to understand this, and a large number of papers have been adjudged spoiled, and not counted. Beyond this, Democratic supporters in the city are alleging widespread ballot rigging. Since the adoption in Mongolia of a capitalist society (whichever party has been in power) some people have become very rich, but the poor have become poorer. This has been exacerbated this year by high food price inflation, and in the shanty towns the people voted overwhelmingly for change and in favour of the Democrats. Angered by the election results, the people have taken to the streets.

Upwards of 100,000 demonstrators have crammed into the main square, and violence has erupted. The MPRP headquarters has been attacked, ransacked, and set on fire. Cars have been overturned, and the riot police have turned out in force, but have been unable to contain the crowds. As night fell we heard that young supporters of the Communists were moving towards the square, and there were reports of attacks on foreigners. I retreated to the Guest House, but as I did so I could hear more shouts and screams from the square, and further reports that the army had been called to quell the violence.

I scribbled the above notes last night, as the post office had been closed and I had no access to the Internet. I awoke around 3am to the sound of gunfire. I heard at least two shots in the small square where the Guest House is located. An army vehicle slowly circled the square, its searchlight scanning the buildings, before rumbling off.

July 2 – morning

This morning we went to take a look. The Communist Party headquarters has been completely gutted, and there are burnt cars littering the surrounding area. The President has announced a state of emergency, there is a curfew tonight, and apparently a blackout on foreign news reporting. The Internet has been turned off at the Post Office, and all the internet cafes are closed. I am writing this in the Ulaanbataar Hotel, which is right next to the Communist Party HQ, but untouched.

I don't know if the violence has spread to the ger districts on the outskirts of the city, but I am grateful that the children are down at the Camp. In a few minutes I will call Didi and find out what her plans are. I feel really sad.

July 2 – later

Just spoke to Didi. She was in the main square until midnight, and saw the army move in and use live bullets. She saw people shot, and blood in the square. The army were pulling people off the streets. Didi was grabbed, but managed to escape back to her apartment. She went back to the square at 6 this morning, and picked up spent bullets. Someone photographed her, and was arrested. Didi's photo was taken by the police. She was with two other people and as they moved away the other two were arrested and beaten.

All is quiet now, but the crowd is growing again, and there is evidence of a gathering of riot police. We are going back to the

Guest House, and will meet Didi later. I was concerned about her, and asked her if she wanted us to go to over to her apartment, but she says she is fine. That is a relief. She is a tough woman.

July 2 – evening

We met Didi later in the day to go to the Camp. She has heard that at least five people were killed the previous night, with another 150 plus injured. About 700 people are said to have been detained. No foreign correspondents are being allowed to file reports, and the Internet is off throughout the City. It seems that only the UB hotel has full access to the outside world. The state of emergency is to last for at least four days.

Didi told me more about her attempted arrest – she had gone into a narrow street behind the MPRP HQ to pick up bullets. She was grabbed by two soldiers who tried to pull her towards a van. She was able somehow to drag them back into the main street into general view, and shouted to people to see what was happening. Somebody started to take photographs, and Didi was released and instructed to hand over the bullets she had picked up – she did, but kept some of them. She knows that the army will deny that live bullets were used. I myself had seen used cartridges as I had moved away from the scene earlier the same day. They were trying to clean the blood from the steps of the post office.

I have to say it was with great relief that we drove away from the City towards the Camp, at which we arrived in the late afternoon. The children were delighted to see us, and nobody in the Camp seemed to know anything about the violence in the City centre – it had certainly not spread into the ger districts, for which we were grateful.

As it was the first full day in the Camp (three weeks after they all should have been there), we had the Camp Opening Party round a bonfire on a warm evening. There was a lot of singing and dancing, and I was especially pleased to see Zorig there, sober, and playing the keyboard that had been provided out of the proceeds of a yoga day organised by Brenda in January. I hope he stays okay, because he is basically a good man, and the children like him.

It felt very good finally to be back where I had spent most of last summer, and I experienced once again the happiness of simply being with the children.

July 3

We spent the morning playing with the children in the Camp – football, frisbee, badminton etc. Brenda spent some time doing craft work with some of the girls, using materials we had sent out earlier in the year, and then helped the older girls do their washing in the river – which they do every day. She has a particularly good relationship with Ariunzea, who speaks good English (in spite of, and not because of, my efforts last year!), and they chatted together for a long time.

In the afternoon I went for a walk up the hill behind the Camp, with Ankhar, to pick up a message from Didi, who had said she might want me to go to a meeting with her the following morning. As we stood at the top of the hill lightning flashed and thunder crashed. We raced down the hill, but not quickly enough – the heavens opened, and by the time we got back to the Camp we were completely soaked. Within minutes the Camp was awash. Presumably because of the heavy rain through June the ground just cannot take any more water.

Didi arrived in the early evening with all the children's dancing costumes, as they had asked to dance for Brenda and me during our all too brief stay in the Camp. Everyone was very disappointed that it proved just not to be possible, as the rain simply refused to give up. In fact it rained right through until about 7 in the morning, and if this happens on many more days they will have to close the Camp and once again retreat back to UB.

July 4

The meeting Didi had mentioned related to the new Lotus Centre and was to take place at 9:30, with a follow up meeting at 3 in the afternoon. As this was our last day we therefore, much too soon, had to say our goodbyes to the children. Chinzorig was quite emotional, and I walked with him to the edge of the camp, away from the others. I promised him I would come back every year, and asked him to carry on with his schoolwork, so as to achieve his ambition of becoming an architect. He said little, but cried, which I had not seen from him before. We hugged, and then walked back to say goodbye to the others. Brenda said that some of the girls had laughed at him because he had cried, but I believe he is strong enough to cope. I had told him last year that it was good to show his emotions, and perhaps he had remembered that.

The other children, although sad to see us go, were all fine, apart from poor Galaa who retreated behind a ger to hide his tears.

Later on I thought about Chinzorig's reaction to me this time. All of the others had been pleased to see me, but he seemed really to have missed me. He never knew his father, and is he looking upon me as some sort of replacement? I have to be careful, because clearly I can never fulfil that role in my brief visits, and nor would I want to. But what can I do to help this one child achieve his enormous potential? It is something I need to talk to Didi about.

On the way back to the City Didi showed us the site of the proposed new Centre, which is in a wonderful location about 20 kilometres from UB, but close to a good sized village which has a regular bus service into town. It is a much safer, healthier, location than they are in now, and the children will benefit hugely. About 35% of the fundraising has already been achieved, but the rest will be hard work. However, it is essential: the existing Centre is too cramped (some of the children have had to sleep three to a bed); there is no possibility of drilling for fresh water; theft is rife

– food stocks and coal were stolen from the Centre last winter, when the temperature dropped at one point to minus 44C; basic sanitary facilities are lacking; and, perhaps most importantly of all, the existing buildings have a limited life span, and are going to have to be replaced in any event. The new site offers space, water, better surroundings, and generally a much improved environment in which to care for and bring up the children.

As we arrived back in UB there was still a very obvious military presence. Troops with guns were patrolling in small groups, and there were armoured vehicles on the edge of Sukhbaatar Square. We met a Dutch guy who has been living in Mongolia for twelve years, and who told us that he had heard shots and screams the previous night, after the curfew. Walking through the Square we were apparently followed by a plain clothes policeman. Didi is a well known figure in UB, easily recognisable, and her photo had been taken on the night of the riots. It is not impossible that the police were looking out for her. We spoke to someone else who had acted as an election supervisor, and who had heard that the MPRP were offering cash at the polling booths to people who voted for them.

Brenda and I met Nyamaa for lunch at Ananda, Didi's vegetarian cafe. Nyamaa, a ger mother last year, is now teaching English in one of the state schools. She lives in a ger in one of the shanty towns, with her sister, mother and grandfather, who are all dependent on her. Her grandfather had made me a pair of traditional Mongolian slippers, but their ger had been flooded the previous night, and the slippers had been damaged. She had bought me a replacement pair in the market, but was clearly disappointed. It's not hard to understand why I am so fond of these people.

And so tonight, after the last meeting, we have dinner with Ben, and then fly home. It has been another amazing experience. A mixture of emotions – love for Didi, the children, and the country;

respect for the majority of its people; shock that such peaceful people should be so moved by frustration and bitterness that they turn to violence against the government; and anger at the over-reaction of the police and army.

With all this, Mongolia is now in my blood, and I shall be back.

UPDATE

Since arriving back in England in July 2008 I have heard:

- that Chinzorig has changed schools, and is now working hard again;
- that Gantaluk failed to get into the dance and drama college, and is losing interest in dance, although he is still producing beautiful artwork;
- that Six Senses have as yet been unable to agree terms to build a resort in the hot springs east of Ulaanbaatar;
- that Didi has completed the purchase of a rundown apartment to be converted into a Guest House which will be staffed by Lotus school leavers, and which will help to provide not only employment opportunities, but also funding for Lotus' operational costs. Once repaired and decorated, the Guest House will be fitted out free of charge by the Swiss charity "Globetruckers", which was introduced to me by David Allen;
- that Galaa is now living happily at The Potato Farm where he works hard on the land planting and growing potatoes. He was becoming increasingly isolated at the Centre, and is much happier now that he has a 'real' job to do. There is one house mother living here with him, and they both return frequently to the Centre, so that he is still in touch with the other children;
- that Inkhzaya and Inkhchumick have been taken back by their mother, and are now again living in the environment where Inkhzaya was sexually abused. There is nothing Didi can do about this;
- that Didi has been awarded the Order of Australia in the 2009 Australia Day honours list, for her work with the street children of Mongolia.

APPENDIX

OUT IN THE COLD: THE STREET CHILDREN OF MONGOLIA – AN EXTRACT

1997

Fourteen-year-old Uer wanted to show me the crayon picture she had drawn. It was divided in two parts. On one side was a popular soap opera star, Sterlita, sleeping in a bright bedroom with pink curtains and fluffy pillows. The other frame showed Uer (pronounced "Er") and her friends, in a stairwell. Her friends were propped up against one another, sleeping. Uer sat on the stairs staring out of the drawing, head in hands.

"That's you?" I asked, pointing to the obvious figure. "Yeah," she smiled back the beginnings of a blush. "I like Sterlita." Then she snatched the picture back to fill in some details. Uer has a thick black braid wrapped around her right shoulder, smoky almond eyes and clear skin. Bright, but with a weary sadness about her, she's one of a rapidly growing number of street children struggling to survive in Ulaanbaatar, the capital of Mongolia.

I met Uer at the apartment of Gabrielle Dowling, an Australian volunteer with AMURTEL, an international relief organization. Dowling (known by her spiritual name, Didi Kalika) and her group of Mongolian volunteers have worked with street children in Ulaanbaatar for about three years. They feed and wash the children and administer superficial medical treatment. Dowling's group also set up a small house with baking and sewing facilities where street girls live with volunteers, learning skills which may help them stay off the street.

"The circumstances in Mongolia are very, very difficult right now," said Dowling. "Prices are going up and families can't manage, which means a lot of kids go to the streets."

A UNICEF report on the social conditions in Mongolia published last April links a depressed economy with increased alcohol abuse and increased violence against women and children. According to the report, most of the street children are from single-parent families. Several of the children I met had siblings with different fathers.

One 11-year-old boy wants to go back to his mother, who is now living with her fourth husband. He has two sisters and all three of them have different fathers. But, he said, there is no way he can return. His reasons are very similar to those of many of the children I spoke with – his stepfather abused him regularly.

Another boy, 12-year-old Naranbat, talked about his situation. "My stepfather always hit my mother and my brother and me," he said. "So we ran away. My brother and I went to live with our aunt in Ulaanbaatar and my mother went back to my stepfather. But my aunt's son always hit us so we left and went to live on the street. It's rough but it's better than being beaten". All of the children's stories were similar – a stepfather, father, sibling or grandparent's violence forced the child out of the house.

There is one government-run home and school for homeless children in Ulaanbaatar – The Trust Center. But both services and staff are questionable according to some activists and government social workers. Many of the children I spoke with lived at Trust at one time or another but decided the streets were better. The reasons most commonly cited – beatings and sexual abuse by both teachers and other students.

"We're tough," said 12-year-old Batbayar with a mannish grin. "We sleep in the stairwells even in the winter. It's better than the hole. The kids in the hole get sick, but not us. We're tough."

The "holes" that many Mongolian street children call home during the long winters are maintenance chambers in the steamy bowels of Ulaanbaatar's sewer system.

The children spend their winters nestled up to hot water pipes. Their forays above ground to steal money or food, or for the girls to sell their bodies, provide the perfect opportunity for infection. So some children, like Batbayar, prefer to tough it out above ground during the long, very cold winter.

In mid-July the city is crackling with anticipation for the biggest annual festival in Mongolia – Naadam, a time for horse-racing, archery, wrestling and partying. The street children at Dowling's house are also excited. Four of them come to show her the new clothes they've stolen from a department store to wear for Naadam.

"What can I say?" asks Dowling, exasperated. "Should I tell them stealing is bad and kick them out? They want to look good for Naadam like everyone else."

The city of Ulaanbaatar is also cleaning up for Naadam . Officials from the National Children's Foundation have teamed up with foreign missionary groups to run a two-week summer camp for the street children. The two-week stint just happens to coincide with Naadam.

"I can't say they did it on purpose," says Dowling. "But that's what it looks like, doesn't it? They don't want the foreign tourists to see the children and get a bad impression of the city."

* * * *

Thirteen-year-old Sarantunga boasts she has 35 boyfriends. "All of the streetboys love her," says her friend Battsetseg. "She's very popular."

Sarantunga has been on the streets for about three years and she knows the ropes of survival. There are fewer street girls than boys in Ulaanbaatar, but their lives are layered with an extra difficulty – prostitution.

"I usually approach men near the cinema," says Sarantunga. "I get five or six thousand tugrik ($12 or $14) from them and then on the way to where they want to have sex, I run away."

I asked if they ever catch her. "Sometimes they do and then they beat me. Once I got two black eyes and a bloody nose. I'm afraid sometimes."

Sarantunga had a vague understanding of pregnancy and no clear idea of sexually transmitted diseases.

"I don't understand how a baby could get inside of me because babies are so big and I'm so small," she said looking puzzled. "Last month I got my period for the first time and I didn't know what it was and I got really scared and started crying. Now I know I can get pregnant but I still don't see how it's possible."

Sarantunga also talked of her fear of being a girl of the streets. "We have to sleep outside and the men bother us. They want sex. It's very difficult."

Dowling said that the girls are often raped and they have little protection. "Even the police officers, who are supposed to be protecting them, rape them," said Dowling.

I asked Batbalsan, the Lt. Colonel in charge of Children's Services for the Ulaanbaatar Police Department. "There's no official record regarding this," he said. "If this was a real fact, the girls would have to come tell me about it, then I could do something about it."

"Also, this not only happens with the police," he continued. "In some schools it happens. Perhaps the teachers or police officers are young and they fall in love with the young girls. There are lots of love stories. Perhaps at first it's rape, but then they fall in love."

"The girls' situation here is not really looked at by society," said Dowling. "So many girls are abused by so many people – the police, teachers and men in the street. There should be separate government facilities for the girls. You can't just lump all the children together. "Due to the added pressure of life on the streets as a female, many of the street girls have serious emotional problems. In Dowling's apartment, Uer's 13-year-old friend, Uyanga, also wanted to show me her drawing. But it wasn't on paper. It was carved on the soft underskin of her left forearm.

"The boys seem to be doing okay," said Dowling. "They kind of keep a humorous attitude about their situation. But the girls have a tougher time. They're much more emotionally effected."

Dowling's housing and education project currently can accommodate only seven girls. She hopes to expand the facility, but worries about having any impact whatsoever on girls like Sarantunga, who have been on the street for a long time. Although Dowling encourages Sarantunga to visit her apartment whenever she needs help, she won't let her live in the house.

"Sarantunga has been on the street for a long time and she's used to that life. When I've let her stay here before she's stolen things and come and gone as she pleased," said Dowling. "She's not used to parental authority, she's used to the freedom of the streets and it's very difficult for me to help her, except in superficial ways, because I can't change her mentality.

"I'm trying to take girls who are just new to the street into the house and help them before the street culture takes over their minds. It's really frustrating but it's all I can do right now." Sarantunga wants to be a pianist when she grows up. But most likely she will end up in prison. Most of the street children are very adept at shoplifting and many have been caught and punished. When they turn 16 they become adults, according to the law, and then the punishment becomes a prison sentence.

"Many of the children spend their time stealing because they want nice clothes and sweets. They're children," said Badamhand, a child welfare advocate. "So most of them will end up in jail. They have no future and it's very sad."

"This society needs to change," she continued with a long sigh. "We need to get back to our roots, our culture and the values we had. It will take a long time. First, we need to pay attention to the children."

Kristine Weber

Acknowledgements

I would like to acknowledge the help of the following:

- My partners at Maxwell Winward LLP who allowed me to take the time off and experience the most rewarding summer of my life.
- My friend Brian, whose idea it was to write the blog.
- My Swedish friend Jan, who (with help from his girlfriend) designed and constructed my website in the space of seven days.
- Jacqui, who tirelessly corrected all my errors as I converted the blog into this book.
- Brenda, without whose love and support I would not have gone to Mongolia in the first place.